SAMPLING *and* CHOOSING CASES *in* QUALITATIVE RESEARCH

SAGE has been part of the global academic community since 1965, supporting high quality research and learning that transforms society and our understanding of individuals, groups, and cultures. SAGE is the independent, innovative, natural home for authors, editors and societies who share our commitment and passion for the social sciences.

Find out more at: **www.sagepublications.com**

Connect, Debate, Engage on Methodspace

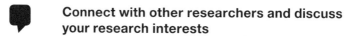 **Connect with other researchers and discuss your research interests**

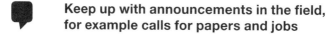 **Keep up with announcements in the field, for example calls for papers and jobs**

 **Discover and review resources**

 **Engage with featured content such as key articles, podcasts and videos**

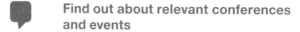 **Find out about relevant conferences and events**

www.methodspace.com

brought to you by

NICK EMMEL

SAMPLING *and* CHOOSING CASES *in* QUALITATIVE RESEARCH

a realist approach

Los Angeles | London | New Delhi
Singapore | Washington DC

Los Angeles | London | New Delhi
Singapore | Washington DC

SAGE Publications Ltd
1 Oliver's Yard
55 City Road
London EC1Y 1SP

SAGE Publications Inc.
2455 Teller Road
Thousand Oaks, California 91320

SAGE Publications India Pvt Ltd
B 1/I 1 Mohan Cooperative Industrial Area
Mathura Road
New Delhi 110 044

SAGE Publications Asia-Pacific Pte Ltd
3 Church Street
#10-04 Samsung Hub
Singapore 049483

Editor: Jai Seaman
Assistant editor: Anna Horvai
Production editor: Ian Antcliff
Copyeditor: Jennifer Hinchliffe
Proofreader: Nicola Marshall
Indexer: Martin Hargreaves
Marketing manager: Ben Griffin-Sherwood
Cover design: Francis Kenney
Typeset by: C&M Digitals (P) Ltd, Chennai, India
Printed in India at Replika Press Pvt Ltd

© Nick Emmel 2013

First published 2013

Library of Congress Control Number: 2013932701

British Library Cataloguing in Publication data

A catalogue record for this book is available from
the British Library

ISBN 978-0-85702-509-8
ISBN 978-0-85702-510-4 (pbk)

To Inna, Elena Rosa, and Nina Clara

CONTENTS

LIST OF TABLES

LIST OF FIGURES

ACKNOWLEDGEMENTS

Theory does not fall out of data and this book has not fallen out of my experiences of doing research, although each of my research projects is represented in one way or another throughout the book. I am grateful to the UK Economic and Social Research Council (ESRC), which funded three methods research programmes of which I have had the good fortune to be part: *Developing Methodological Strategies to Recruit and Research Socially Excluded Individuals and Groups* as part of the Research Methods Programme; *Connected Lives*, part of the Real Life Methods Node of the National Centre for Research Methods; and *Intergenerational Exchange*, part of Timescapes, the ESRC's Qualitative Longitudinal Initiative. Within these programmes the colleagues with whom I do research have all contributed. There are far too many to mention here, but one of the arguments rehearsed in Chapter 7 is the way in which interpretation and explanation are produced through discussion and debate within research teams. This book is no different in this regard.

While my colleagues can take comfort from my insistence that the ideas in this book are my own, they must accept at least a small part of the responsibility through encouraging me, putting forward their ideas, and arguing their corner in many memorable hours of interpreting and explaining method and substance in our research together. I would particularly like to thank Kahryn Hughes, Joanne Greenhalgh, Andrew Clark, Adam Sales, and Lou Hemmerman. Sarah Irwin, Bren Neale, Jennifer Mason, and Mike Savage listened to my thinking about choosing cases and provided insightful comments. James Newell has always acted as wise interlocutor between qualitative and quantitative methods. Lisa Buckner guided me through the mysteries of quantitative sampling and answered my questions. I thank them all for their time and patience. Joseph Maxwell, Graham Crow, Michelle O'Reilly and Karen Henwood responded to my requests for hard-to-access papers and books with generosity. Martyn Hammersley read and commented on a very early draft of what is now Chapter 4. His incisive comments were invaluable, my thanks.

I have received wonderful support from Patrick Brindle, Jai Seaman, and Anna Horvai at SAGE. I am enormously grateful to one anonymous reviewer and one reviewer who made himself known, Bob Carter. Of course, for all their support, these are my interpretations of choosing cases in qualitative research. But, one person can take some of the blame for what is written here, Ray Pawson. It was he who came up with the alliteration in the title of the book and enthused about this project since I first had the idea of writing a realist account of sampling in qualitative research. His comments on drafts have been incisive, witty and occasionally irreverent – the support anyone writing a book needs in my view. Finally, my partner Inna and our daughters Elena Rosa and Nina Clara have shown infinite patience. My thanks and love to them.

ABOUT THE AUTHOR

Nick Emmel teaches research methods and the sociology and social policy of international health and health care at the School of Sociology and Social Policy, the University of Leeds. He has conducted extensive research in the UK and India interpreting and explaining processes of vulnerability, with a focus on inequalities and inequities in health. He is particularly interested in the methodological challenges of access to hard-to-reach individuals and groups and how these processes contribute to insight in our research. He has published extensively on these issues, including with Kahryn Hughes in the *SAGE Handbook of Case Study Research* (edited by David Byrne and Charles Ragin, SAGE, 2009). He was a co-investigator in the Real Life Methods Node of the ESRC's National Centre for Research Methods and in Timescapes, the ESRC's Qualitative Longitudinal Initiative.

INTRODUCTION: FROM SAMPLING TO CHOOSING CASES

I am really not sure the verb 'sampling' does justice to the acts of choosing cases in qualitative research. Sampling in the sense most often used in research refers to two activities: first, defining a population from which a sample will be drawn and of which the sample will be representative; and secondly, ensuring that every person or thing from this predefined population has the chance of inclusion that is greater than zero and can be measured. Neither of these rules, which statisticians from Sir Arthur Lyon Bowley (1906) to Stephen Gorard (2007) insist upon in sampling strategies, applies to the choosing of cases in qualitative research. On the contrary, and as I will show in this book, what happens to sampling in qualitative research is best described through inverting these two rules and thinking about measurement in very different ways.

Nonetheless, I am obliged to use the term sampling because this is the way most writers on qualitative research methods talk about selecting units to be included in research.

If I find the term sampling not fit for purpose, the strategies proposed by various authors to implement sampling are so diverse as to confuse utterly. There is considerable divergence of views about where one should start in collecting a sample; one author will strongly advocate using a strategy of convenience sampling, the next will caution against its use, ever. One writer will make the case for theory emergent from data in decisions about where to turn next to select participants to a study. The next advocates bringing well developed research questions and ongoing intellectual work to these sampling strategies. The ways in which the sample in the research is reflected in the claims from the research is yet another area of contestation. For some, the sample is a bearer of grounded theory, emergent and discovered through coding. For others, claims as theories are anchored in the sample's real-life experiences in a grounded way. As for sample size, there are authors who advocate a quite specific number for a particular kind of study, and others who argue sample size is not the issue, but how researchers convince their audiences with the cases they are able to collect given the resources available to them.

Three cases of sampling: theoretical, purposeful, and theoretical or purposive

Given this divergent advice there can be little surprise that sampling is reported in qualitative studies in rather ambiguous ways. The terms used to describe sampling strategies, theoretical, purposeful, and purposive, have wide ranging and occasionally contradictory meanings. Quite often these differences of meaning do not seem to be appreciated. During the writing of this book I found the following quotes in papers reporting qualitative research in peer-reviewed journals. (I've chosen not to cite the authors because I don't want to demean anyone, and where necessary I've restructured sentences so a quick Google search for the sentence within inverted commas won't find the original source). Consider the following:

1 We sampled theoretically using a grounded theory approach (Glaser and Strauss, 1967; Strauss and Corbin, 1990) ...

or

2 We sampled theoretically and purposefully (Morse, 2007; Patton, 2002) ...

or

3 Our sample is theoretical or purposive (Charmaz, 2006; Mason, 2002).

I chose these three quotes because I feel they have useful pedagogic purpose; each outlines dominant theories about the methods that are legitimate grounds for generating knowledge about the social world in qualitative research. Also emphasised through this investigation of strategies for sampling is the considerable epistemological diversity among the relatively small number of methodologists who have considered sampling in qualitative research. To make some sense of this diversity the first part of this book presents three cases in three chapters.

The boundaries of the first case (Chapter 1) are explained and broadly defined through a common name, theoretical sampling, and, in turn, a common epistemological assumption that theory is discovered, emergent, or constructed from empirical observation of interaction. This empiricism, as Chapter 1 will trace, holds various methodologies together that use the term 'grounded theory'. But this case also reports and interprets considerable variation across these methodologies. This is exemplified in comparing the authorities cited in the first quote, which bring together two quite different ways in which theoretical sampling is understood and realised in grounded theory approaches. While certain underlying assumptions of grounded theory have stayed much the same since its inception in the landmark methodological account of *The Discovery of Grounded Theory* written by Barney Glaser and Anselm Strauss (1967), one area where there has been a significant change in approach is in theoretical sampling. The two accounts of grounded theory cited in the first quote characterise the role of the researcher implementing theoretical sampling very differently. For Glaser and Strauss (1967) theoretical sampling is achieved through the medium of the open, theoretically sensitive researcher – the *tabula rasa* (blank slate) that has become the pejorative criticism of this formulation of grounded theory – but which for Glaser and Strauss provides the methodological device of an objective distance they required between researchers and researched, object and subject, and which allowed for the positivist twist in their account of qualitative research.

Wider debates in the social sciences in the latter part of the twentieth and early twenty-first centuries are reflected through this investigation of theoretical sampling. In Chapter 1, I outline the ways in which debates in grounded theory methodologies have diverged between the positivism I have already described in the work of Glaser and Strauss (1967) and constructivist grounded theory (Charmaz, 2006).

I will return to constructivist grounded theory shortly, but a way-mark between these two incommensurate claims for legitimate ways of knowing the world is provided by Strauss, with his new methodological ally, Juliet Corbin (Strauss and Corbin, 1990). The blank slate is replaced with one chalked up with directions. Researchers are encouraged to have preconceptions about that which is to be studied. The chance of discovery is replaced by plans and strategies. As Strauss and Corbin (1980: 46) emphasise, quoting Louis Pasteur, 'chance favours only the prepared mind'. Serendipity and being prepared to discover are a considerable distance apart, so too are the two versions of grounded theory cited in the first quote.

The second quote is connected by a term, this time purposeful sampling, which both Janice Morse (2007) and Michael Quinn Patton (2002) use to describe sampling strategies. Yet, the way in which both of these methodologists use this term is quite different. For Morse (2007) purposeful sampling is a method or strategy applied to focus the theoretical sample in grounded theory. Morse, as I will show in Chapter 1, reworks the positivist and objectivist version of grounded theory. For her, purposeful sampling is a strategy nested in theoretical sampling to focus and test emergent concepts that follow on from the comparison of incidents in convenience sampling.

This strategy is quite different from sampling purposefully, as elaborated by Patton (2002). Here pragmatic judgements are brought to bear in showing how a purposeful sample derives its logic and power from the selection of information rich cases. These cases are chosen by the researcher to provide insight into issues of central importance to the research and always with an eye on the audience of the research, resources, and the best story to be told.

Convenience plays no part in Patton's definition of purposeful sampling. These are key differences in the ways in which purposeful sampling strategies are proposed and in particular how researchers' judgements inform the choosing of cases in the research. Michael Quinn Patton's formulation of purposeful sampling strategies is the subject of Chapter 2.

The third quote once again makes reference to grounded theory, emphasising its influence across qualitative researching. And, as I mentioned above, stressing the significant differences within the idioms of grounded theory.

A move often referred to as the reflexive turn in the social sciences is included in Kathy Charmaz's (2006) constructed grounded theory. This is expressed through the privileging of discourse and language as the precondition for the being of things. Theories are co-constructed through the reflexive acts of researchers and participants.

The second methodologist cited in the final quote, Jennifer Mason (2002), takes a quite different position towards reflexivity, which is worked out in her account of theoretical or purposive sampling. This is the focus of the third case presented in Chapter 3. The boundary of this case is another long-standing methodology in qualitative research – analytic induction. Mason (1996, 2002) argues that researchers explicitly bring wide ranging intellectual work to their research. Their decisions about whom or what to sample hinge on an interplay between this work and the empirical contours of the sample, which in turn inform sampling strategically and organically. There is no turn to reflexivity in this account of theoretical or purposive sampling, it has always been part of these strongly interpretative and analytic inductive strategies.

The organisation and purpose of Part One of the book

The first part of this book can be read as a methodological investigation across three different traditions, which I have broadly outlined above: first, the empiricism of grounded theory and theoretical sampling across a continuum from positivism to constructivism; secondly, the practicality and judgements of the pragmatic researcher implementing purposeful sampling strategies; and thirdly, the strongly interpretative analytic induction of theoretical or purpo-sive sampling. One feature considered in the first three chapters are that all these three cases locate the real, as social phenomena that exist independent of our accounts of them, through outlining a particular relationship between evidence, meaning and mental phenomena (hereafter theory or ideas). And each of these cases provides quite different accounts of how sampling should proceed in qualitative research, and the justification for these.

These three chapters may be read as primers of three cases of sampling strat-egy, as theoretical, as purposeful, or as theoretical or purposive. Another way to consider the first part of the book is as a synthesis, from which methodological and practical insight can be gained towards thinking differently about sampling in qualitative research. This is, I suggest, the pedagogy of Part One.

A realist case for sampling in qualitative research

Part Two of this book presents a realist approach to sampling. Like Joseph Maxwell, who has recently published a realist approach for qualitative research,

I think 'realism can do some serious and important work' in qualitative research (Maxwell, 2012: viii). This is the work of practical methods and techniques that arise from the ways realists think the world is and the claims realism makes to legitimately investigate the world. Methodology, Malcolm Williams suggests, is the 'bridge between [this] metaphysics of the social world and its methods' (in Letherby et al., 2013: 114). Much of the discussion in Part Two is about a methodology of realist qualitative research and its implications for methods and techniques, including the practical challenges of sampling, working out the relation between ideas and evidence as cases, and justifying sample size in research.

To this end the argument for a realist methodology of sampling draws on examples from research across the disciplines of the social sciences. Much of this research does not explicitly claim to be using a realist methodology. I have interpreted and explained them in this way. In some cases, as noted in the acknowledgements, opportunities have arisen to discuss my re-interpretation with the original authors, but in many cases this has not been practical. I hope that the ways in which I have presented the work of others reflects the methodological sophistication I have seen in their work.

One reason for seeing realism in the methods of others is, I think, because most researchers are realists. As Ray Pawson and Nick Tilley (1997: 56) observe, 'claiming to be "realist" can sometimes feel like choosing to bat on the side of the "good"'. Indeed, cast around for long enough and there really does seem to be no end to the realisms being used in research, from social to structural, via subtle and scientific, it sometimes feels like there are as many versions of realism as there are realists researching. Given that one of the key features of realism, as I will discuss below, is that our explanation of the real can only ever be provisional, this is probably inevitable. The realism I use in this book draws predominantly on critical and scientific realism. I discuss the implications of this choice in much more detail in Chapter 4, for the moment presented below in five propositions is the scientific realism I adopt here.

Proposition One: 'Social reality is not simply captured by description or ideas, but is richer and deeper' (Malcolm Williams in Letherby et al., 2013: 105). Reality is stratified and our theories about the social objects we investigate refer to actual features and properties of the real world. These properties include real and relatively enduring mechanisms, which Roy Bhaskar (2008: 221 – parentheses in the original) considers to be 'nothing but the powers of things. Things, unlike events (which are changes in them) persist'. Powers, liabilities, and dispositions are an essential part of any realist explanation of sampling in qualitative research. These have causal efficacy, they have an effect on behaviour, and they make a difference. Amongst these powers are the researchers' concepts of that which they are investigating. But, as Maxwell (2012: 13) contends, 'our concepts refer to real phenomena, rather than being abstractions from sense data or purely our own constructions'.

Proposition Two: Accounts of real phenomena, including the sample in research, are weak constructions. The best we can say of these is that they raise consciousness about social objects we seek to interpret and explain.

Proposition Three: A realist investigation zigzags between ideas and evidence. It neither starts with specific empirical instances (induction), nor from general statements (deduction), but from fragile ideas (or more grandly, bold yet naïve conjectures) to be tested and refined through engagement with evidence. Realist research works out the relation between ideas and evidence. Sample choices and the ways in which these are worked and reworked as cases throughout the research allow us to explain to some degree this zigzag route of investigation.

Proposition Four: Reality, particularly of the social world, is only ever relatively enduring. As discussed in Proposition Three, our interpretation and explanation are efforts to work out the relation between ideas and evidence. These relations we present as models (or less grandly – Ideas on the backs of envelopes – Greenhalgh et al., 2009), which can be transferred from one complex system to another to be tested and refined. These can never be described as typical or critical cases (as would happen in analytic induction) because interpretations and explanations are constituted of irreducible inner deliberation and public outworking in open social systems, as Margaret Archer (2000) contends.

Proposition Five: Interpretations and explanations – the insiders' perspectives and the outsiders' understandings – cannot be separated and are always provisional. They are implicated in theories of the middle range, which seek to explain what works for whom, in what circumstances, and why (Pawson and Tilley, 1997; Pawson, 2006, 2013). They provide explanations as to how particular generative mechanisms (M) – the causal powers discussed in Proposition One – act on social regularities in specified contexts (C) to bring about observable outcomes (O); or as Ray Pawson and Nick Tilley put it more elegantly, C+M=O. We test and refine these theories through repeated and critical engagement within the scientific communities of which we are part and through further investigation.

The organisation of Part Two of the book

This book is divided into two parts. The first part I have discussed above. It presents three cases in three chapters of methodological arguments for theoretical, purposeful, and theoretical or purposive sampling, alongside examples of these methodologies of sampling in practice. In Part Two the focus is on a realist approach to sampling in qualitative research, although I have cause to return often to methodological debates raised in the first part of the book.

Chapter 4 addresses the basics of a realist strategy of choosing cases. Considered here are the internal and external causal powers, or generative mechanisms that shape research. The next three chapters deal with the three key considerations in a realist sampling strategy. Chapter 5 considers purposive work and how presuppositions as bold yet naïve conjectures are brought to bear on the choice of cases. These purposeful choices are the focus of Chapter 6, which considers how a realist casing strategy differs from constructed and typical cases, and how cases are transformed in research. The methodological strategy of casing, the working out of the relation between ideas and evidence to extend interpretation and explanation in the research, is discussed in Chapter 7. Chapter 8 brings together the key methodological debates from Part One of this book, along with the methodology of a realist sampling strategy in qualitative research, to consider sample size. Chapter 9 presents choosing cases in qualitative research: a realist approach.

PART ONE
THE CASES

1

THEORETICAL SAMPLING

This chapter presents the first of three cases in the book, theoretical sampling in grounded theory. Brought together here are methodological accounts spanning nearly 50 years, from the ground-breaking writings of Barney Glaser and Anselm Strauss in *The Discovery of Grounded Theory* to much more recent constructivist accounts of grounded theory. The debate about how theoretical sampling should proceed in a piece of research reflects wider methodological debates about how we generate legitimate knowledge about the social world. There is significant diversity discussed in this chapter. The boundaries of the case are defined by an enduring principle of grounded theory approaches within this diversity; theory emerges or is discovered through empirical investigation in which the decisions and implementation of theoretical sampling play a key role.

The discovery of grounded theory

Barney Glaser and Anselm Strauss were concerned that qualitative research was seen, up to the 1960s in the United States, as largely an enterprise to verify theory. It was often used as a preliminary exploratory effort to provide insight and hypotheses to be tested more rigorously through quantitative methods. These methodologists wanted to show that qualitative research was an enterprise in its own right, capable of providing scientifically robust accounts of the social world. It was not merely a useful precursor to quantitative research. Qualitative research was quite capable, with the right methodological strategies, of generating credible, reliable, and useful theory derived from the qualitative investigation of social interactions.

This theory, Glaser and Strauss (1967: 32) suggest, is a 'theory of process' which is an ever-developing and never-perfected product. Through a rigorous method of constant comparison, qualitative research has the ability to generate theory at different levels of generality. Theory may be empirical and substantive, such as patient care, race relations, or the relationships in an organisation. And at a higher level of abstraction, theory can be formal and conceptual social theory, of stigma, deviant behaviours, or authority and power as examples. Together these empirical and formal theories are described by Glaser and Strauss as theories of the middle range, drawing on the work of Robert K. Merton. For Merton (1968: 39) middle-range theory is:

> Intermediate to general theories of social systems which are too remote from particular classes of social behaviour, organization and change to account for what is observed and to those detailed orderly descriptions of particulars that are not generalized at all. Middle-range theory involves abstractions, of course, but they are close enough to observed data to be incorporated in propositions that permit empirical testing.

The challenge of the discovery of grounded theory is to systematise a method that allows for a move from empirical observation to the generation of grounded (middle-range) theories and the testing of these theories through empirical observation. These observations are of meaning making, its modification and interpretation between people in their social interactions, a theory of symbolic interaction. Grounded theory, through its investigation of micro-empirical interaction, can discover theory that falls somewhere between "'minor working hypotheses" of everyday life and "all inclusive" grand theories' (Glaser and Strauss, 1967: 33 – emphasis in the original). Instrumental in this discovery and testing of theory is theoretical sampling.

Theoretical sampling

Theoretical sampling is set to work to generate theory in qualitative research through the investigation of the empirical social world. The 'grounded' in grounded theory is where the theory is to be found, it is observable and can be interpreted from the behaviour of groups in their everyday social interaction. Herbert Blumer (1978: 38) employs a metaphor of 'lifting the veils', which obscure the area of group life that the researcher intends to study. And, in a further metaphor, research is 'digging deep (in these group lives) through careful study'. Grounded theory respects and stays close to these empirical domains in its research.

To make visible the hard-to-see elements of the empirical social world requires three different dimensions to be addressed in theoretical sampling, according to Glaser and Strauss. These are the controlling influence of emerging theory, the open and theoretically sensitive researcher, and constant comparison.

The controlling influence of emergent theory

Emerging theory is central to processes of theoretical sampling, in which the researcher:

jointly collects, codes, and analyzes … data and decides what data to collect next and where to find them, in order to develop … theory as it emerges (Glaser and Strauss, 1967: 45).

The emphasis here is not only on the methodological process of sampling, but on the central role of this process in the generation of theory. As such, we cannot talk about a theoretical sample. Theoretical sampling can neither be reified to a thing – the identification by researchers of a person, an organisation, document, or research instrument to be sampled – nor can the sample be identified ahead of the research. Instead, the researcher is continuously guided by emerging theory as to where to go next in search of their sample. Structural (or practical) concerns are not the guide to identifying the sample; rather it is the impersonal criteria of emerging theory. As Glaser and Strauss (1967: 47 emphasis in the original) observe:

> The basic question in theoretical sampling … is: *what* groups or sub-groups does one turn to *next* in data collection? And for *what* theoretical purpose?

In conceptualising the sample in this way a grounded theory approach is distancing itself from the sampling strategies of quantitative researching and from qualitative researchers whose aim is to verify theory. Qualitative researchers, Glaser and Strauss (1967: 30) argue, neither need to 'know the whole field', nor are they seeking to represent all the facts in the sample through random selection to ensure every member of a given population has an equal chance of being in the sample. In using theoretical sampling, researchers are not seeking a perfect representation of a concrete situation under study. They are aiming to generate general categories and their properties for general and specific situations and problems, through the acts of writing memos and coding.

Theoretical accounts are tied to particular social phenomena through these memos and codes. But, in emphasising the impersonal way in which theoretical sampling is linked to emergent data, the aim of grounded theory is to remain objective through maintaining a distance between researchers and researched. The account of theoretical sampling in early grounded theory holds to a strongly positivist approach. The characterisation of the researcher as open and theoretically sensitive emphasises this positivism.

The open and theoretically sensitive researcher

An approach to sampling driven forward by emergent theory rather begs the question, where does one begin? The answer lies, in part, in the personality and temperament of the researcher, according to Glaser and Strauss (1967).

The grounded theorist is an open and theoretically sensitive researcher. At the outset researchers begin with a partial and unelaborated framework for their research. They will have only a basic outline of the problem to be researched. Researchers must guard against making decisions about what to sample based on a preconceived framework. Openness to discovering concepts in the field is seen as important in ensuring a researcher is able to identify and refine concepts in the early stages of the research. The concepts that inform these early stages of fieldwork sampling are no more than a general sociological knowledge and an understanding of the general problem area of the research. The researcher, Glaser (1978: 44) suggests, can go anywhere, talk and listen to anyone, read anything with nothing more than the overarching problem in their mind, but that researcher must be 'capable of conceptualisation'.

Researchers capable of doing theoretical sampling are characterised by their receptiveness to emergent theory in the field. A researcher with 'complete openness is often more receptive to the emergent (theory) than others with a few pre-ideas and perspectives' (Glaser, 1978: 46), although it is grudgingly accepted that researchers do come to research with some theory. But this theory must be articulated and tested against the empirical data and emergent theory in the research. Most theory is induced through observing, seeing, hearing, reading, and recording particular incidents. The researchers' open minds are directed towards the coding of observations and the fashioning of emergent theory. The search in early theoretical sampling is for these incidents, which are sampled as they are found. So, for instance, Glaser and Strauss (1967) talk about how they might sit at a nursing station on a hospital ward watching the nursing staff at work, or talk about the research area with key informants. The conversations are broad, the observations general.

At this early stage in the research, it is the sampling and exploration of various incidents to discover underlying uniformities and varying conditions that are of interest. Given that the early research is based on such openness, false starts and starts that do not quite get at the concepts under investigation are inevitable, but these are soon corrected by the constant comparison of theoretical sampling, Glaser and Strauss (1967) assure us.

Constant comparison

The third controlling influence in theoretical sampling is constant comparison. Table 1.1 identifies each of the different kinds of comparison Glaser and Strauss advocate in theoretical sampling. The linear progression from the sampling of incidents, occurring in the first stage of theoretical sampling, is mediated by theory, described as concepts, as the research progresses. Constant comparison seeks an ever-increasing refinement of emergent theory.

Table 1.1 Constant comparison in theoretical sampling: an overview (after Glaser and Strauss (1967) and Glaser (1978))

Stage	Theoretical sampling activity	Purpose
1	Comparing incidents with incidents	Establishing underlying uniformity and varying conditions
Open coding and analysis to discover concepts		
2	The concept to more incidents	Testing concepts towards enriching their explanation, elaboration, and the generation of further concepts
3	Concept to concept	Establishing the best fit of concepts to a set of indicators, drawing on hypotheses between concepts to develop theory
Choosing groups to control the scope and conceptual level of the theory		
4	Outside comparison of the substantive area (Once it is safe …)	Going outside the data, to literature for instance to strengthen the 'stabilised' grounded theory
5	Outside comparison beyond the substantive area	A must for generating formal theory

Theoretical sampling becomes much more selective, focussing on the concepts identified in the researchers' emerging theory.

The initial focus of constant comparison on observable incidents such as a particular behaviour, like Glaser and Strauss's (1967) example of the ways in which nurses respond to dying patients for instance, assures ample data will be collected which can be coded. From these codes, memos describing theoretical concepts can be written, which when elaborated allow for the theoretical sampling of individuals and groups to the research. Theoretical sampling is far more difficult than collecting data with pre-planned groups; individuals and groups selected theoretically require that decisions are made informed by thought, analysis, and search. The sample's ongoing inclusion in the study is for a strategic reason, to test emerging theory. Here again Glaser and Strauss differentiate themselves from their nemesis, the verifier of theory. Evidence, they suggest, is not collected because it will accurately describe or verify some preconceived theoretical position, nor is the researcher selecting groups because they show difference in a particular variable. The logic is not one of: 'I plan to sample this group because they use this service, and this group because they do not use this service'. These rules of evidence hinder the discovery of theory. Groups are chosen because the data they produce relates to a particular category in the research. The search is for groups that display the category under investigation in different situations. Thus, in their study of the *Awareness of Dying*, Glaser and Strauss

(1965) observe the interaction between nurses and their patients in hospitals, the home, nursing homes, ambulances, and even in the street following trauma, and through these the various interactions between nurses and dying patients. Such diversity of investigation allows for observation of the similar and diverse properties of categories.

Strategies of constant comparison and their purpose

There are a further three considerations in the choice of which group to sample next. First, the scale of generality the researchers wish to achieve with their theory. What is the scope of the theory? Does it relate to a particular setting, or is the research making claims for other settings too? If Glaser and Strauss's 1965 study *Awareness of Dying* discussed in the last section had just been conducted in a hospital, then the theory would have been confined to hospitals alone. The scope of the theory would have been limited by these choices.

The second sampling choice is whether to minimise or maximise similarities in data categories. These conceptual categories discovered in the early research are transformed into hypotheses to be tested with similar and diverse groups. The purpose of this strategy in the research is threefold. It 'forces', to use Glaser and Strauss's term, the researcher to generate categories, their properties, and interrelations in their emergent theory. Similar data collected in similar groups verifies the usefulness of the categories, aids in the generation of basic properties, and establishes the conditions in which the emergent theory will apply. Understanding these conditions of context allows the researcher to make predictions about the generality of the theory to other settings. These claims can be made stronger and the emergent theory refined through the strategic sampling of similar data categories between maximally varied groups. The emergent theory's scope is extended.

An overarching logic of grounded theory as described by Glaser and Strauss (1967) is the linearity of its implementation. This is the reason for numbering the stages in Table 1.1. Iteration between the joint collection, coding, and analysis of data happens within each stage. Nonetheless, while they accept some overlapping of the stages, the rigour of the discovery of emergent theory rests on theoretical sampling proceeding from stage to stage. The basic work of establishing concepts, properties, and categories through minimising the difference between the groups sampled in the research precedes strategies of maximisation. The early work of openness and categorisation are the precursors to emergent theory. Maximum variation is sampled to bring out:

> the widest possible coverage of ranges, continua, consequences, probabilities of relationships, process, structural mechanisms ... all necessary for elaboration of theory. (Glaser and Strauss, 1967: 57)

However, such a wealth of insight requires these methodologists to accept that they might have to revisit their early data collection, as their understandings of phenomena change. So, for instance, Glaser and Strauss (1967) note how through observing the ways in which Malayan families care for their dying relatives in Malaysia, they were obliged to go back to their own data on US families. Their conceptual framework had characterised US families as ignoring their dying relatives who they regarded as a nuisance. But a re-examination of the data led them to identify 'not-so-observable' phenomena in their data, leading them to discover several different ways in which US families care for their dying relatives.

The purpose of constant comparison is to extend empirical theory into the realm of formal theory. This theoretical sampling can only be done, according to Glaser (1978), when the emergent and empirically generated theory has been stabilised. Then, at last, the researchers can make their weary way to the library in search of other studies and other theoretical accounts or sample dissimilar and non-comparable groups. These comparisons provide the researcher with further instances to facilitate explanation at the higher conceptual level of formal theory and extend the scope of the findings from the research.

Grounded theory in action in a study of the awareness of dying

An important influence in the development of grounded theory was the study *Awareness of Dying* conducted by Glaser and Strauss (1965), in which they note that they have written theory on almost every page. Our interest here is not the theories discovered, however fascinating, but the methods used to arrive at these theories, and in particular the decisions made about who and what to sample in the research. In an appendix Glaser and Strauss (1965) discuss their methods of data collection and analysis. The first notable feature, which appears to sit at odds with the position taken in *The Discovery of Grounded Theory*, is the amount of work that was done before entering the field. They discuss a preliminary stage in their data collection, which 'governed further collection and analysis of data' (1965: 286). In this section, they discuss how their understanding of their research interest, an awareness context of death and dying, was 'foreshadowed' by personal circumstances and experiences. These authors describe how these circumstances and experiences informed theory development in the early research. First, a state described as 'closed awareness' and then a 'mutual pretence awareness' experienced by Strauss during the death of his mother. A while later he was involved in 'an "elaborate collusive game" designed to keep a friend unaware of his impending death (closed awareness)', (Glaser and Strauss, 1965: 287). Glaser, too, had recently been through the experience of his father's death and had gained sociological insight about death expectations through the ways in which professionals had talked with family about his father during his dying days.

As a preliminary to data collection, Glaser and Strauss (1965: 287) had 'systematically worked out the concepts (and types) of death expectations and awareness contexts and the paradigm for the study of awareness concepts'. This guided preliminary data collection. But also evident are the openness and theoretical sensitivities of the researchers to investigate social interactions:

> Fieldwork allows researchers to plunge into social settings where the important events (about which they will develop theory) are going on "naturally". The researchers watch these events occur. They follow them as they unfold through time. They observe the actors in the relevant social dramas. They converse with or formally interview the actors about their observed actions' (Glaser and Strauss, 1965: 288).

From memos written in the study of the *Awareness of Dying*, theory was ever present in the minds of the researchers. They made decisions from the outset, first looking at sites where patient awareness of dying was minimised – premature baby services and those dealing with comatose patients, then quick dying – the intensive care unit, and then where staff expected death to be slow such as cancer services. The study is one of constant comparison where groups are sampled by the logic of the emerging analytic framework with the aim of:

> verifying (in diverse settings) our initial and later hypotheses, of suggesting new hypotheses, and providing new data either on categories or combinations of categories. (Glaser and Strauss, 1965: 289)

The purpose of this comparison is to increase the scope of their study through searching out the structural conditions in which hypotheses can be tested, while at the same time delimiting their theory and its generality. Claims are bracketed by the approach to constant comparison taken in the research. Their intention is always to formulate substantive theory faithful to the empirical situations they have observed. This faithfulness, Glaser and Strauss (1965: 276) observe, 'cannot be formulated by merely applying a formal theory to the substantive area'.

A reworking of grounded theory

In 1990 Anselm Strauss and a new collaborator Juliet Corbin published a reworking of the methodology of grounded theory. The contribution they make to theoretical sampling has a rather different feel to it. In part, the clue as to how these authors wanted to develop grounded theory is in the sub-title to their book. *The Basics of Qualitative Research* (Strauss and Corbin, 1990) is about procedures and techniques. It is a practical response to a number of problems, as they perceived them, with the original methodological approach, including theoretical sampling.

In *The Discovery of Grounded Theory* little attention is paid to resources in research. While procedures were discussed, their practicality was often elusive; these feel like a promissory note to not worry unduly, you will soon find your bearings when searching for your sample informed by emerging theory. Indeed, as one reads this account one's thoughts reflect back to halcyon days (if they ever existed) when undergraduate and Masters dissertations did not have a fixed hand-in date, PhD research didn't have a time limit of three years to complete, and research funders were not overly concerned whether the outputs from research made an impact. We are constantly obliged in research to reach decisions before we start any research about its resource implications; crudely, how long it will take, how much researcher time we will need, and how much it will cost. Answers to these issues are never open ended. They are most often fashioned and expressed through the priorities of funding bodies, the institutions with which we study and do research, and pressing social need. The times when there were opportunities for open-ended research that starts with nothing more than an overarching problem in mind are long gone, if they ever existed.

In contrast to the impractical, almost mystical tone of Glaser and Strauss's *The Discovery of Grounded Theory* and Barney Glaser's *Theoretical Sensitivity* (1978), the work of Strauss and Corbin (1990) is, as Kath Melia (1996: 375) has observed, 'rather formulaic' and rule-like in approach. In a reworking of their earlier work, Corbin and Strauss (2008) list 15 rules for doing theoretical sampling, for instance. The claimed intent of both these accounts is that the techniques and procedures they lay out will make learning grounded theory easier.

Making decisions in the design of the research

Alongside these pedagogic issues and an acceptance of the importance of resource issues in the design and implementation of research, Strauss and Corbin (1990) also re-shape the role of researchers in theoretical sampling. The open, theoretically sensitive researcher, essential to theoretical sampling advocated by Glaser and Strauss (1967) in *The Discovery of Grounded Theory* and discussed above, is required to be much more reflective and proactive in designing the research. There is now recognition that researchers must have more than just an overarching problem to address. They are now called upon to spend time developing research questions, research goals, and plan how these will be achieved with the resources they have available to them. 'The research question in a grounded theory study', Strauss and Corbin (1990: 38) observe 'is a statement that identifies the phenomenon to be studied.'

Social phenomena are characterised as features of the social world that can be described in some way or another. These descriptions use variables and categories. While they may be seen as inadequate, they are the concepts available to researchers at the beginning of their research that start to frame a study. Corbin and Strauss are edging towards this framing of the study in their re-working of grounded theory. They observe that in designing a study, consideration is given to:

> concepts pertaining to a given phenomenon (that) have not been identi-fied, or aren't fully developed, or are poorly understood and further explanation on a topic is necessary to increase understanding (Corbin and Strauss, 2008: 25)

They stress that not all concepts relating to a phenomenon are emergent or discovered in the research. Some must be conceived of and worked out by researchers in planning the research. But they will inevitably be recognised as inadequate.

The fiercest critic of this change in emphasis and approach was Barney Glaser (1992) who, in a rather disparaging manner, described this new methodological development in grounded theory as 'full contextual description'. Going on to note that:

> The research question in a grounded theory study is not a statement that identifies the phenomenon to be studied. The problem emerges and questions regarding the problem emerge by which to guide theo-retical sampling. Out of open coding, collection by theoretical sampling, and analysing by constant comparison emerge the focus for the research. (Glaser, 1992: 25)

Glaser went further, accusing Strauss and Corbin of misconceiving the original principles of grounded theory. He argued that the new strategy abandoned theoretical sensitivity, and therefore theoretical sampling. The untainted emer-gence of theory through the observation of incidents was replaced, in Glaser's view, by the 'forcing' of emergence through strategies that introduce precon-ceived and substantive understandings of phenomena into the research design.

Accepting reflection in choosing samples

Strauss and Corbin (1990) were responding to new ways of thinking about doing qualitative research. The demand for objective distance between researcher and researched, which had informed the earlier methodological account of grounded theory had to a degree been superseded by recognition of the researcher as a reflective agent in the research. Decisions about whom or what to sample are no longer entirely guided by emergent data, but are made, at least in part, by researchers.

The changes Strauss and Corbin (1990) and Corbin and Strauss (2008) made to grounded theory do not punctuate the equilibrium of grounded theory with totally new thinking, however. Their approach is gradualist. This reworking of grounded theory still holds to the principles of theoretical sampling laid out in *The Discovery of Grounded Theory* through sampling theoretically relevant incidents, which are described as:

> what people do, their interactions and action in the range of conditions that give rise to these actions and interaction and its variation; how conditions change or stay the same over time and with what impact; also the consequences of either actual or failed action/interaction or of strategies never acted on (Strauss and Corbin, 1990: 177).

Theoretical sampling is still firmly anchored in observable empirical data and guided by symbolic interaction and constant comparison. Like in Glaser and Strauss's initial formulation of grounded theory, sampling aids the researcher to discover and relate relevant categories, their properties, and dimensions. But, while pedagogically the presentation is rule laden and structured, the approach proposed by Strauss and Corbin (1990) is

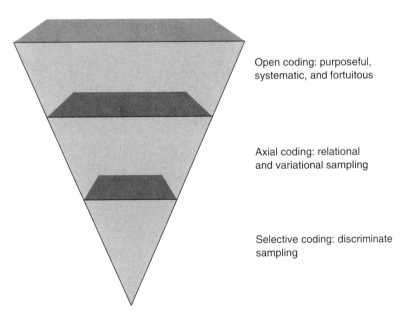

Open coding: purposeful, systematic, and fortuitous

Axial coding: relational and variational sampling

Selective coding: discriminate sampling

Figure 1.1 Focussing the researchers' understanding of the phenomenon under investigation: the funnel-like structure of sampling and coding in grounded theory as described by Strauss and Corbin (1990)

less positivist than its predecessor. This reworking accepts the ways in which researchers bring theory to their research, particularly in the early stages. The emergence of theory from micro-empirical observation, nonetheless, continues to direct sampling through much of the research. These changes have an impact on the shape of the research. Grounded theory loses its linear structure of discovery, as suggested earlier in Table 1.1, the strategies for sampling proposed by Strauss and Corbin (1990) and Corbin and Strauss (2008) take on a funnel like character (Figure 1.1), in which sampling becomes more focussed as the research progresses through open, axial, and discriminate coding and sampling. And, as we see in the next section, the way in which theoretical sensitivity is conceptualised changes as well.

Theoretical sensitivity and the focussing of sampling, coding, and emergent theory

For Strauss and Corbin (1990) initial concepts and observations contribute to the planning of research, drawn from literature, existing research, and experience, which allow for the selection of sites or groups with reference to the main research question. These general considerations also facilitate decisions about the kinds of data, such as observations or interviews, for instance, that 'best capture(s) the kind(s) of information sought' (1990: 179). Furthermore they allow for detailed methodological plans to be made about how the study will proceed. It is suggested, for instance, that:

> If studying a developmental or evolving process, you might want to make some initial decisions about whether to follow the same person over time or different persons at varying points. (1990: 179)

As can be seen, the emphasis on initial decisions in this account is rather different to that of Glaser and Strauss (1967) in the earlier formulation of grounded theory.

The relation between refining the sample and theoretical sensitivity is also presented rather differently from the earlier version of grounded theory. For Strauss and Corbin there is an increasing focus to theoretical sampling, with coding and analysis aligned to a growing theoretical sensitivity. This is a different characterisation of theoretical sensitivity to the one defined in the initial version of grounded theory. Open, axial, and discriminate coding and sampling guide the research, or act as a springboard for future sampling decisions. In this process the researcher becomes more theoretically sensitive, it is no longer an attribute of the researcher, but intrinsically linked to the process of researching.

Sampling in open coding

Developing this theme of the increasing theoretical sensitivity of the researcher, Strauss and Corbin suggest that in the early research researchers are at their least sensitive, their early fieldwork requires sampling in open coding. This aids discovery and the naming and categorising of phenomena. Openness rather than specificity guides the search for the most relevant data and instances. These will provide the greatest opportunity for insight into the phenomenon and facilitate data comparison. Strauss and Corbin (1990) suggest three techniques of open sampling. These may be used alone or in combination in the early research.

First, sampling may be purposeful. Sites, persons, or documents are chosen deliberately because they have a bearing on the categories, dimensions, or properties of the social phenomenon under study. Strauss and Corbin describe, for instance, how in an investigation of hospital equipment they identified various 'properties or dimensions' that they thought were important. Amongst these dimensions, or dependent variables, were size, cost, and status. They chose to sample the biggest, costliest, and highest status equipment, the Computerised Axial Tomography (CAT) scanner, because it 'maximized opportunities for discovering differences made by such machinery to patient care and the work of medical personnel' (Strauss and Corbin, 1990: 184).

The method of purposeful sampling offers opportunities for exploring difference. The second method proposed, systematic sampling, exposes more subtle differences, Strauss and Corbin (1990) claim. Sampling is done through proceeding from one person to the next, from place to place, or document to document, searching out incidents and events of interest to the study. A systematic sampling approach increases the chance of uncovering similarities and differences. Through going from unit to unit in a hospital to observe head nurses at work they identified differences in organisational structure between units that provided a useful basis for comparison in the study.

The third of the methods of sampling in open coding is fortuitous sampling. Unexpected insights from the fieldwork are incorporated into analysis. This is a method of chance. Strauss and Corbin (1990: 184) emphasise the importance of the researcher's 'open and questioning mind'. But this is also a mind aware of the significance of events or incidents to the study, which suggests more than an ability to ask questions like What is this? What can this mean? in a merely open way. Researchers are bringing theoretical presuppositions to the research that mediates their theoretical sensitivity.

Sampling in axial coding: relational and variational sampling

Sampling in open coding exposes variation and process and encourages theoretical sensitivity. Sampling in axial coding, aided through the researcher's ever increasing theoretical sensitivity, seeks to make more specific the theoretically relevant concepts (categories and sub-categories) in the research. Juliet Corbin suggests that sampling in axial coding goes hand-in-hand with open coding (Corbin and Strauss, 2008). Their earlier account of theoretical sampling deals with each of these strategies separately. I consider axial coding separately here as this aids in understanding what each part of the sampling strategy is used for in the research.

Axial coding is undertaken to relate different categories identified during sampling in open coding. Sampling is directed systematically and purposefully towards uncovering and validating the relationships between categories. Its purpose is to explain how categories relate across 'conditions, contexts, actions/ interactions, and consequences' (Strauss and Corbin, 1990: 196). The aim is to relate these categories to this 'paradigm', or emerging theory, through sampling on the basis of theoretically relevant concepts.

Sampling in axial coding happens through both chance and choice. At each step along the way the purpose of axial coding proceeds through analysis and hypothesis testing of emergent theory. Sampling in axial coding is a strategy that recognises the likelihood of any two conditions, or contexts, actions or interactions, or consequences being the same are slight. Sometimes, Strauss and Corbin (1990) suggest the researcher may even manipulate the research experimentally through varying the dimensions of properties of the phenom- enon, through sampling at different times of the day for instance. The pur- pose of sampling in axial coding is to 'find as many differences as possible at the dimensional level of data' (Strauss and Corbin, 1990: 185) through inves- tigating the relationships between categories and sub-categories and finding variation and process between these.

Sampling in selective coding: discriminate sampling

The researcher is now at their most theoretically sensitive, having repeatedly analysed, categorised, and sampled on the basis of theoretically relevant con- cepts through sampling in axial coding. Discriminate sampling is employed to validate statements about relationships, fill in categories, and form theory. It is directed and deliberate, a series of choices used to verify the emergent theory in the research. It may require returning to units that have been sampled in the research to ask new questions, or seeking out of new contexts to test the- ory. Negative cases that do not express the categories at all may also be sam- pled. All of these are used to test theory. As Strauss and Corbin (1990: 187) note, these are 'a crucially important and integral part of grounded theory'. Hypotheses are tested against the data and inform each step of the coding, analysis, and sampling in the research.

The grounded theory sample of empirical reality

The link between analysis and sampling is emphasised in the increasing focus of the sampling strategy outlined by Strauss and Corbin (1990). I have suggested a funnel-like character to this proposed method in Figure 1.1 on p. 21. Corbin chooses a different simile, likening the processes of sampling/coding/analysis in the research to an assemblage of blocks towards the building of a pyramid (Corbin and Strauss, 2008). Whatever way up you choose to see the structure of the sampling strategies, the aim is increasingly refined theory from its discovery or emergence predicated on empirical observation of social interactions.

These interactions are, as Corbin and Strauss (2008) observe, fluid, and complex. In keeping with the ontological assumptions of symbolic interaction, it is the creation and change of the world by human beings in their ceaseless actions and interactions, whether rational or not, that are the focus of sampling and enquiry. The theoretical sampling of empirical units that display, or fail to display the actions/interactions as categories and sub-categories under investigation allow for the discovery and building of theory. Sampling of empirical regularities and associated coding and analysis make possible the testing of emergent theory through seeing empirical data as real. As Corbin and Strauss (1990: 187) observe:

> Though not testing in a statistical sense, we are constantly comparing hypotheses against reality (the data), making modifications, then testing again. Only that which is repeatedly found to stand up against reality will be built into the theory.

The constant comparison proposed by Strauss and Corbin (1990) equates empirical observation with an external reality. This, however, sits uncomfortably with the observations already made about the ways in which this reworking of grounded theory opened the door to a degree of researcher reflexivity. As discussed, this is proposed at two levels, first in the theoretical work done in shaping the initial research problem or question, and secondly through the ways in which the theoretical sensitivity of the researcher is conceived of as a process driven forward through sampling/coding/analysis. For Strauss and Corbin theoretical sensitivity is not an inherent characteristic of the researcher.

In part, we may see the grounded theory method proposed by Strauss and Corbin (1990) as an attempt to resolve a central ontological challenge of grounded theory, what counts as reality. It is a challenge that remains unresolved in both *The Discovery of Grounded Theory* and in its reworking. As Kathy Charmaz (2009) observes, grounded theory brought together two contrasting philosophical and methodological traditions. Barney Glaser studied

Objectivist grounded theory	Constructivist grounded theory
Assumes an external reality	Assumes multiple realities
Assumes discovery of data	Assumes mutual construction of data through interaction
Assumes conceptualisations emerge from data	Assumes researchers construct categories
Views representation of data as unproblematic	Views representation of data as problematic, relativistic, situational, and partial
Assumes neutrality, passivity, and the authority of the observer	Assumes the observer's values, priorities, positions, and actions affect views

Figure 1.2 A comparison between the foundational assumptions of objectivist and constructivist grounded theory (after Charmaz, 2009: 141)

with Paul Lazarsfeld and Robert K. Merton at Columbia University, while Anselm Strauss was supervised by Herbert Blumer at the Chicago School (of Sociology). These disparate traditions of positivism and pragmatism/symbolic interaction, as Charmaz (2009: 129) goes on to observe, placed grounded theory on 'somewhat unsteady ontological and epistemological grounds and planted the seeds of divergent directions of method'.

This divergence is exemplified in the ongoing debates about theoretical sampling in grounded theory. Charmaz (2009) suggests that the methodological accounts of grounded theory now sit along a continuum between an objectivist grounded theory and a constructivist grounded theory. The foundational assumptions of each of these polar positions are outlined in Figure 1.2. What is considered to constitute reality clearly discriminates between the two diverging traditions. It is to an examination of the implications of these when considering theoretical sampling in the ongoing debates in grounded theory that I now turn.

Theoretical sampling in an objectivist grounded theory

The work of Janice M. Morse (1991, 2007) exemplifies the objectivist approach in modern grounded theory. This approach draws extensively on the work of Glaser (1978), in which he restated and to some degree clarified the original conception of grounded theory. Morse insists that theoretical sampling can only happen through an open theoretically sensitive researcher whose focus, even at the outset, is guided by receptiveness to incidents of phenomena in the field. Thereafter theoretical sampling is guided by concepts, which are emergent theories derived from the coding and analysis of empirical data.

26

This approach assumes that conceptualisations emerge from the data, and that everything going on in the research scene is data. As Glaser (2002) asserts, 'all is data'. Morse (2007: 231), states that it is inappropriate to select participants using variables or categories, or as she puts it, 'demographic characteristics such as age, gender, ethnicity, economic status, and so forth'. The criteria for selecting a theoretical sample should be the conceptual and informational needs of the study. We might question quite what the differences between these are, but what is being emphasised is the emergence of theory over imposition of theoretical constructs.

In pursuing this theme, Morse asserts that using a random sampling strategy based on a variable is not an appropriate way to select a sample. This will provide a representative sample of the population, but it will only be representative of the demographic characteristics used in selecting the sample, she argues, which will tend to provide insight into common experiences that cluster around the mean of a normal or skewed distribution. Less common experiences, represented at each of the tails of the distribution are poorly represented. Qualitative data, according to Morse (2007), should be thought of as being represented by a more rectangular distribution, with purposeful choices made to ensure that all experiences are represented in the account.

Neither should a stratified sample be considered in which participants are selected in proportion to their frequency in the population. To emphasise this point, Morse (2007) argues that because a given population is 40% Caucasian, 20% Black, 20% Hispanic, and 20% other, the sample should not be made up of eight Caucasians, four Blacks, four Hispanics, and four others, providing a sample of 20 to the study. A far better approach is that of the convenience sample. This allows researchers to go to the places or sites where they think they are most likely to see the social actions and interactions they are interested in investigating. Through openness and theoretical sensitivity they are likely to identify potential categories through enquiry, coding, and analysis.

This objectivist approach to theoretical sampling assumes that empirical regularities are the external reality and the representation of data is unproblematic. Any deviation from openness and theoretical sensitivity will inevitably lead to conceptual blindness, Morse (2007) argues. The appropriate ways to proceed in identifying a purposeful sample is through sampling participants who are going through a critical juncture in a particular trajectory of a phenomenon. Researchers choose particular relationships and different stages in the developing relationships. This is a deliberate strategy of selection based on what is understood about the phenomenon from its empirical investigation and the coding of these data that precedes the purposeful theoretical sampling strategy. Morse (2007: 238) claims to be 'solving problems detective-style, looking for clues, sifting and sorting, and creating a plausible case'.

The assumption that the researcher is neutral and authoritative in the research is emphasised through a prescription to seek out these optimal rather than average experiences. Objectivist approaches advocate an inherent selection bias, predicated on empirical emergence. The best cases are selected for analysis in the first instance. This is done because:

> By using the worst – or best – cases, the characteristics of the phenomenon or experience we are studying become most obvious, clear, and emerge more quickly and cleanly' (Morse, 2007: 234).

Only once these worst or best cases have been explored and the researchers know what characteristics to look for in the data, can they move on to sample and interrogate less optimal examples. This selection bias means that a focus can be maintained on identifying the best empirical cases to discover and test theory through the external reality of the empirical world.

In this account Morse (2007) emphasises the comparative, emergent, and open-ended approach to theoretical sampling. Objectivism, and indeed positivism, is the key underlying assumption in this approach. Maintaining a distance between observers and observed, alongside theoretical sensitivity and openness are further key coordinates of this theoretical sampling. Janice Morse does suggest that the original account of openness suggested by Glaser and Strauss (1967) might need tempering a little. A middle course, which characterises the researcher as less passive is appropriate:

> The researcher should not go into the setting with an agenda of using some theoretical model, and sort the data accordingly. Neither should the researcher enter a setting blindly, without a vast compendium of (social science) knowledge (Morse, 1994: 4).

The researchers are neither forcing data into preconceived theoretical positions, nor are they a passive bystander. What is more, despite the feeling of 'thou shalt' and 'thou shalt not' in Morse's methodological prescriptions, she, like Glaser and Strauss (1967), emphasises the creative approach of grounded theory research. This insistence on flexibility, while apparently resisted by Glaser (2002) in his increasingly grumpy rejections of changes to his formulation of grounded theory, opens up opportunities for a description of grounded theory as constructivist. This sits at the opposite end of the continuum to an objectivist approach as described in Figure 1.2.

Theoretical sampling in constructivist grounded theory

Recent accounts of theoretical sampling (Charmaz, 2006, 2009; Clarke, 2009; Bryant, 2003) have advocated a constructivist grounded theory. This approach, echoing and indeed amplifying Strauss and Corbin's (1990) method of how research and theoretical sampling starts, explicitly recognises the researchers' reflexivity is a point of departure for the research. As Kathy Charmaz (2006) explains, theoretical knowledge, hunches, and hypotheses are necessary starting points in planning a research project. What is more, emergence and discovery give way to the construction of theory. Adele Clarke (2009) describes the researchers' analysis within the research as moving beyond the knowing subject searching out silences, absences, structural discourse, and hidden positions that resonate through participants' accounts. It is accepted that researchers bring theoretical constructs to the research to co-produce theory with their participants.

For some, including Barney Glaser (2002), this is not grounded theory at all, but qualitative data analysis. But despite Glaser's objections, Charmaz and colleagues do see their reformulation as grounded theory. They note the significant critique of positivism that has happened since the first rendering of grounded theory fifty years ago (Charmaz, 2006, 2009; Bryant, 2003), their aim is to reposition the methodology of grounded theory. Charmaz (2000: 510) seeks to add:

> another vision for future qualitative research: constructivist grounded theory. Constructivist grounded theory celebrates first hand knowledge of empirical worlds, takes a middle ground between postmodernism and positivism, and offers accessible methods for taking qualitative research into the 21st century. Constructivism assumes the relativism of multiple social realities, recognizes the mutual creation of knowledge by the viewer and the viewed, and aims toward interpretative understanding of subjects' meanings.

The middle ground between postmodernism and positivism may be disputed territory, but what connects these poles is empiricism. For Kathy Charmaz it is a place where theory is constructed. This construction privileges participants' narrative accounts of experiences rather than material observation of interaction. To get to this middle ground requires theoretical sampling with its purpose of directing researchers to the empirical accounts of experiences which allow for data to be obtained through which to develop the meanings and implications of categories. These categories, when full, will reflect the qualities of 'respondents' experiences and provide a useful analytic handle for understanding them' (Charmaz, 2006: 100).

Karen Henwood and Nick Pidgeon (2003) describe this approach to theoretical sampling as theoretical agnosticism, in which theoretical concepts have to earn their way into the narrative of the research. They are always treated as problematic. Researchers must look for the ways in which they are lived and understood. This is the engine of theoretical sampling in constructed grounded theory.

Necessarily, therefore, theoretical sampling does not start at the beginning of the research. It is preceded by an initial sampling strategy, which presupposes that theoretical categories cannot be known beforehand. They are not articulated in the research question, but are constructed through the analysis of data. The only lead as to what should be sampled at this initial stage is a set of criteria to sample particular people, organisations, or settings where the topic of the research might happen. In doing this initial sampling researchers are obliged to both confront preconceptions about the topic under investigation and refine the scope of the topic to be investigated. Access to participants requires a recasting of the topic. Similarly, finding that certain groups interact in a particular way may lead to the research being circumscribed.

Jane Hood (quoted in Charmaz, 2006: 101) describes theoretical sampling as allowing the researcher to:

> tighten ... the corkscrew or the hermeneutic spiral so that you end up with a theory that perfectly matches your data.

This hermeneutic spiral is made up of data collection, coding, memo writing, and theoretical sampling. Theoretical sampling is specific, and systematic, and through this strategy facilitates predictions into where and how data will be found to fill gaps and saturate categories. It is an informed search for statements, events, or cases that will in some way illuminate categories. There is a constant interplay between inductive strategies, forming hypotheses from data, and then deductive investigation to test these hypotheses against the empirical world of the investigation. This abductive strategy, with its constant reference back to the empirical world keeps theoretical sampling moving towards emergent objectives. These, according to Charmaz (2006: 104), include delineating the properties of a category, checking hunches about it and saturating its properties. It allows for categories to be distinguished, and relationships between different categories to be clarified, and finally, Charmaz (2006) claims that abduction will help to identify process.

The focus throughout this constructivist formulation of theoretical sampling is the emergent theoretical categories that allow for the elaboration, checking, and qualifying of these categories. Emerging theory shapes and directs theoretical sampling, which allows for these inductively derived hypotheses to be tested deductively within a topic area and across substantive areas. What is more, this strategy of theoretical sampling allows researchers to return to participants and/or already collected data with more directed and esoteric questions to test hunches. As Antony Bryant (2003: 20) observes:

> The constructivist position would argue that there is a dialogue between the researcher and the research subject – in both senses of the word "subject" – i.e. the person who is the concern of the research, as well as the research area itself.

Throughout this dialogue, what is emphasised is the ways in which researchers, and to a degree participants, co-construct theory from the empirical data collected, analysed, and mimeographed.

Conclusion

A constructivist account of theoretical sampling is considerably removed from the formulation of the grounded theory of Glaser and Strauss (1967). The tracing of the ways in which theoretical sampling have been considered in the evolving methods of grounded theory suggest an increasing accommodation of a constructivist epistemology. The positivist account of theoretical sampling of Glaser and Strauss (1967) has not withstood the onslaught of standpoint and post-structuralist debates intact. As discussed through the historical account of grounded theory in this chapter, there are still methodologists who continue to hold to Glaser's account of objectivist theoretical sampling strategy. But even these have become more accepting of the post-structuralists' reflexive turn in the social sciences. The significant change in approach to theoretical sampling has been to change the characteristics of the open, theoretically sensitive researcher. *Tabula rasa* (or blank slate) was the device in the positivist account of early grounded theory. This may have been rhetorical (Strauss and Corbin, 1990; Charmaz, 2006), but it could not withstand the historical and philosophical attacks on positivism of the last fifty years. Even so, the empirical renderings of theory remain central to all the accounts of grounded theory to the present day. Empiricism is the methodological orthodoxy of grounded theory and theoretical sampling.

The next case, purposeful sampling, considers what insight might be gained through putting aside orthodoxy in favour of a pragmatic approach to sampling. What might we learn from an account in which the main criterion for sampling in qualitative research is the appropriateness of the sampling method, recognising that different sampling strategies might be more or less appropriate in different situations?

2

PURPOSEFUL SAMPLING

The second case is quite different from the first. Much, but not all of the insight into the formulation and description of purposeful sampling arises from applied evaluation research. The researcher's attributes in choosing one of the 14+1 sampling strategies discussed here are judgement and skill applied to what they learn before and during the research. The purpose of purposeful sampling is to select information rich cases that best provide insight into the research questions and will convince the audience of the research. Halcolm, the Sufi Zen interlocutor in Patton's account of purposeful sampling, makes the following observation, 'the evaluator's scientific observation is some person's real-life experience. Respect for the latter must precede respect for the former.' (Patton, 2002: 207) Purposeful sampling is a case of pragmatism in which, as one reviewer has observed, neither theory nor method are overburdened.

Pragmatic sampling

Michael Quinn Patton (1990, 2002) is the most pragmatic of qualitative researchers who, through his interlocutor Halcolm, asks us to ponder 'what we think is real, question what we think we know, and inquire into *how come* we think we know it' (Patton, 2002: A2 – emphasis in the original). Patton describes sampling as purposeful. Purposefulness, as was suggested by Strauss and Corbin (1990) and Morse (2007) in the context of theoretical sampling in grounded theory, suggests a plan. Sampling is instrumental in the research to search out information rich cases to be studied in-depth.

Unlike purposeful sampling in the theoretical sampling of grounded theory discussed in the last chapter, purposeful sampling, otherwise known as judgement or purposive sampling, is designed before the research starts and may be redesigned as the research progresses. It is not driven forward by theoretical categories, but practical and pragmatic considerations. As Patton (2002: 72) emphasises:

> The point is to do what makes sense, report fully on what was done, why it was done, and what the implications are for the findings.

Judgements are made about who or what to sample with reference to the purpose of the study, its context, and the specific audience for the research.

This approach to sampling is based in evaluation, suggesting a practical and applied focus with a concern that:

> evaluation persuades rather than convinces, argues rather than demonstrates, is credible rather than certain, is variably accepted rather than compelling. This does not mean that it is mere oratory or entirely arbitrary ... once the burden of certainty is lifted, the possibilities for informed action are increased rather than decreased (House, 1977 quoted in Patton, 1990: 490).

While much of his focus is on evaluation, Patton advocates the use of purposeful sampling across a continuum of qualitative research from basic to applied research.

The logic of purposeful sampling

The logic and power of purposeful sampling rests on the in-depth study of information rich cases, towards learning a great deal about the research question and the issues considered by the researchers to be of central importance. The researcher decides how to use the sampling strategy. Patton recognises that these decisions are constrained by the resources available to the research. As he observes:

> the (purposeful) sampling strategy must be selected to fit the purpose of the study, the resources available, the questions being asked, and constraints being faced. (1990: 181–182)

This approach of purposeful sampling is not just about practical and achievable considerations. Theory is considered. Basic research in the social science disciplines asks questions that require abstracted and theoretical accounts. Like theoretical sampling, purposeful sampling suggests that researchers carry with them the theoretical positions of their disciplines into their research. Patton acknowledges the importance of the inductive and deductive strategy for generating and confirming theory to basic research. The researcher using purposeful sampling, however, does not focus on the emergence or construction of theory to direct sampling, not least, because the design and implementation of the purposeful sample is considered early in the research, even before researchers have entered the field, and is linked directly to the claims that can be made from the research. As Patton (1990: 181) observes:

> In the process of developing the research design, the evaluator or researcher is trying to consider and anticipate the kinds of arguments

that will lend credibility to the study as well as the kinds of arguments that might be used to attack the findings. Reasons for site selections and individual case sampling need to be carefully articulated and made explicit.

There is a very practical side to qualitative enquiry, in which researchers seek to solve real-world problems. Practical considerations win out over theoretical ones in considering the strategies of purposeful sampling. A pragmatic approach is given precedence over theoretical orthodoxy. Qualitative researchers do not need to have worked out their theoretical position in the research. They make choices for pragmatic reasons, seeking out the richest information, the most appropriate comparisons within the resources available, and always with an eye on the audience for the research. These are the fundamental dimensions of pragmatic purposeful or judgement sampling strategies.

The many strategies of purposeful sampling

Patton (2002) deals with 16 different strategies for purposeful sampling (see Figure 2.1). There are actually 14+1 purposeful sampling strategies Patton recommends. One strategy, convenience sampling, which is discussed in more detail below, is best avoided. The plus one is a combination of any of the other 14. Each of these strategies has a particular logic that may serve a particular purpose. There are, however, six common themes to Patton's 14+1 strategies for purposeful sampling.

- First, researchers make judgements before, during, and after sampling about what to sample and how to use the sample in making claims from their research.
- Secondly, these judgements are made with reference to what is known about the phenomena under study. This includes recognising that much can be learnt from exploring the ways in which phenomena are described through variables, categories, and insight from both quantitative and qualitative research.
- Thirdly, based on what is learnt before the research starts and as the research proceeds, researchers are strategic in selecting a limited number of cases towards producing the most information that is usable.
- Fourthly, researchers are aware of who the audience for their research will be and choose sampling strategies that will produce the most credible results for these audiences.
- Fifthly, these decisions are always constrained by resources, an important consideration but one that should be addressed only after the first four themes are considered. Qualitative researchers would always like to sample more, but have to make choices with reference to time to do fieldwork, budget, and their capacity to analyse the data they collect.

35

- And finally, there are quite different logics to qualitative and quantitative sampling strategies. These differences are exemplified in the purpose of the purposeful sample.

The logic of purposeful sampling lies in the selection of information rich cases, from which the researcher 'can learn a great deal about matters of central importance to the purpose of the research' (Patton, 1990: 169). These cases are worthy of in-depth study because they provide detailed insight. They therefore have a logic and power quite different from that of probability sampling. Neither methods used to ensure an equal chance of every member of a population being included in the study (randomisation), nor methods ensuring that those chosen have the same shared characteristics from a population (representativeness), are of concern in selecting groups for purposeful sampling, although, as will be seen

1	Extreme or deviant case
2	Intensity sampling
3	Maximum variation
4	Homogeneous
5	Typical case
6	Critical case
7	Snowball
8	Criterion
9	Theory based / operational construct
10	Confirming and disconfirming
11	Stratified purposeful
12	Opportunistic or emergent
13	Purposeful random (of small units)
14	Sampling politically important cases
DO NOT USE THIS	Convenience sampling
plus 1	You may mix any of the 14 strategies together to achieve a purposeful sampling strategy that meets your needs. (Patton, 2002: pgs: 243–44)

Figure 2.1 Patton's 14+1 strategies of purposeful sampling

from the discussion of the sampling strategies below, both an equal chance of inclusion and selecting cases with shared characteristics might be applied in purposeful sampling strategies. The use of strategies of randomisation or stratification to select cases are not designed into the study to strengthen claims for the generalisability of the findings from the study, but to seek out cases that give the findings of the research credibility with its audiences.

The first of these 14+1 strategies, extreme or deviant case sampling, focusses attention on the differences between qualitative and quantitative approaches to sampling. Researchers will already have an understanding of the variation in the phenomenon they are investigating. The purpose of this strategy is not to document natural variation through random selection, but to purposefully select cases that are special, troublesome or enlightening. The logic underlying the selection of cases is that lessons may be learned about unusual conditions or extreme outcomes that are relevant to the research. They are special in some way. Researchers make judgements about the cases they can learn the most from.

A study of when battered women kill by Angela Browne (1987) is, for Patton (1990), an exemplar of the use of extreme or deviant sampling. Browne's sample is 42 women charged with a crime of death or serious injury to their partners. These women were recruited through a request from their attorney, based on Browne's evaluation of their history of abuse. As Browne acknowledges, not all abused women kill their partners. Given this, she seeks to identify contextual factors – the impact of violence, the threat of a partner, and the situational and societal variables – that might lead a woman to kill. To this end, she recruited a comparison group of a further 205 women to the study who had been in abusive relationships but did not kill. This comparison group was recruited through media requests and referrals from physicians, emergency departments, and battered women's shelters.

The aim of Browne's psychological study is to 'understand more about the relationships of abused women who kill their husbands, and to understand the dynamics that lead up to the commission of homicide' (1987: 12). Under investigation is the women's action of killing their partners in the context of their positions as victims of abuse, which is defined as a physical assault that may or may not lead to physical injury. In her book, Browne purposefully sampled 11 of the women who killed their partners. They were selected for:

> their representativeness of the sample as a whole and their importance
> in illustrating specific dynamics of the homicide relationship (Browne,
> 1987: 17).

Browne goes on to observe that she selected these 11 case studies to ensure she had sufficient space to present additional and rich detail important to gaining insight into the lived experiences of these women as well as the murder of their partners.

Extreme or deviant purposeful sampling is not the only strategy Browne uses in her research. Purposeful sampling strategies are used in combination. So, for instance, the 205 abused women sampled in the study to provide comparison provide confirming and disconfirming cases that add richness, depth, and credibility to the much smaller sample of 11 women whose case studies are considered in detail. All of these are selected because they are information rich and manifest the phenomenon of partner violence intensely. This is also, on the face of it, a homogeneous sample. All the case studies describe in graphic detail the mounting physical and sexual violence that led up to the event of murder. They reiterate common themes of alcohol and substance abuse, irrational jealousies, and of abused childhoods. But at the same time, considered along other dimensions, as Browne does, the purposeful selection of her sample provides insight into maximum variation. So while many of the experiences of abusive partners are common to all the case studies, there is also detailed description of uniqueness that cuts across the case studies. In the description of the event of murder of the abuser, for instance, Browne (1987) identifies three quite distinct scenarios: where the women are protecting a child; where the women are being assaulted; and where the women know an assault will happen. This purposeful maximum variation sampling allows Browne to present the complexity of the events she is researching.

A further feature of Browne's account points to the ways in which intensity sampling strategies are used. Like extreme or deviant case sampling this requires that the researchers have insight into the variation of the phenomenon they are studying through exploratory research. They make judgements based on this knowledge to select information rich cases. Unlike extreme or deviant sampling, however, the purpose of the selection is not to identify unusual cases, but cases that exhibit the phenomenon of interest intensely. They are excellent or rich examples but they are not unusual.

Samples in qualitative research are invariably small, as will be discussed in detail in Chapter 8. Capturing variation in experience within a small sample creates a particular challenge. How does one compare experiences that are apparently diverse? Patton (1990) suggests that maximum variation sampling turns this potential weakness into strength. As we have already seen from Browne's study of abused women, this strategy purposefully identifies common patterns and core experiences and shared aspects of the cases, while purposefully selecting cases because they varied in quite distinct and marked ways. This strategy allows for the collection of two kinds of data, first detailed descriptions of the uniqueness of the cases, and secondly the shared patterns that cut across cases. These common patterns found in variation provide insight into shared experiences. Purposeful sampling is once again distanced from quantitative approaches. Patton (1990) emphasises that researchers are not trying to generalise findings but are seeking out insights that illuminate both variation and significant common patterns.

In contrast to maximum variation sampling, homogeneous sampling is a strategy with the purpose of investigating a group or sub-group in considerable detail. As Browne shows, it is possible to use this strategy to focus down on a particular part of the sample, which exhibits important variation. Again it is researchers who make the choice as to which cases they wish to investigate. They define the characteristics that describe some particular sub-group in considerable detail – single-parent female-headed households for instance – and purposefully select these cases for intensive investigation.

Typical case sampling exemplifies Patton's (1990) pragmatic approach to purposeful sampling. The typical case may at first sight look like the average. But this is not its purpose. Researchers choose typical example cases to describe and illustrate the phenomena they are investigating to the unfamiliar. Patton emphasises that the sample is illustrative not definitive. A particular problem is deciding what is typical. Key-informants, knowledgeable participants, or some key criteria, derived from the categories that inform understanding of the research, such as projects implemented in a particular kind of place, may be able to help the researchers identify typicality. Exercises that identify typicality in this way may produce quite large numbers of typical cases. Researchers can select a purposeful random sample from these cases. But once again Patton emphasises that random selection is not designed into the study to aid gener-alisation, but to help the researcher make choices about selection. There are no power equation calculations here. The decisions about whom or what to sam-ple are guided by the resources available to the research.

Stratified purposeful sampling extends the typical case sampling approach to include variability that might be seen in a phenomenon. Researchers may find typicality and atypicality in the sample, either while in the field or in their analysis. Or as Patton puts it 'above average, average, and below average' (1990: 240). Each group of cases is fairly homogenous, be these typical or showing maximum variation in some way. The sample size will be small Patton argues (see Chapter 8). This difference sets the stratified purposeful sample apart from stratified random samples in quantitative research.

Critical case sampling once again emphasises the differences between qualitative and quantitative approaches to sampling. A critical case is selected because 'if it happens here it will happen anywhere' (1990: 236). Selecting critical cases does not allow for broad generalisation, but, as Patton suggests, logical generalisation is possible, even from the investigation of a single case. In identifying key dimensions that make a case critical, researchers are able to concentrate limited resources on the in-depth investigation of one or a very limited number of cases to generate as much insight and knowledge as pos-sible, rather than collecting limited insight from many cases.

Identifying a critical case requires that researchers know the key dimensions that are important to their investigation. One approach to identifying these dimensions and finding critical cases, Patton suggests, is snowball or chain sampling. Snowball sampling is characterised by divergence and convergence. Asking well-situated people to nominate people who can provide insight into a phenomenon because they know a lot about it will, potentially, lead the researcher to many different sources. But Patton notes that a small number of key individuals are likely to be nominated often, with their insight being critical to the investigation.

A further approach to identifying cases for investigation is criterion sampling. In this purposeful sampling strategy criteria selected by the researchers are used to identify cases for investigation. These criteria might be identified from quantitative research, such as data from standardised questionnaires for instance, and form the basis for the selection of information rich cases for in-depth investigation. A further way of selecting cases may be that they have met predetermined criteria. Patton (1990) points out, for instance, that researchers may be interested to investigate school children who were absent for over 25% of the time. These cases may be identified from a standardised questionnaire for in-depth qualitative investigation.

Up to this point, Patton's list of strategies for purposeful sampling is guided by pragmatic choices to search out and investigate empirically observable phenomena. The ways of thinking about sampling are informed by the practical applied emphasis of evaluation research. Patton does allow for theoretical and basic social science research in his schema of qualitative research. Theory-based or operational construct sampling is, Patton suggests, a more formal version of criterion sample in which researchers must first work out their theoretical constructs and then look for operational constructs (or real-world examples) of these theories in action. Patton is unsure about this approach, it seems, observing that theory lacks tangibility. It is easy, Patton argues, to determine what people, programmes, organisations, communities, or populations of interest are. Theoretical constructs are much harder to make real in the research. Patton deals with theory in a quite particular way, which is consistent with the other purposeful strategies. Theories lead to constructs as material things that then guide sampling, rather than emerging from the data. Theories, Patton (2002: 238) emphasises, 'do not have as clear a frame of reference'. He then goes on to quote Cook, Leviton, and Shadish (1986: 163) who note that for:

> operational instance of constructs, there is no target population ...
> Mostly, therefore, we are forced to select on a purposive basis those particular instances of a construct that past validity studies, conventional practice, individual intuition, or consultation with critically minded persons offer the closest correspondence to the construct of interest.

In Patton's pragmatic approach to purposeful sampling, constructs can only be sampled if they are real-world examples. That is operational examples of theoretical ways of seeing a particular problem. Researchers may draw on a theory like the classic diffusion of innovations theory, Patton (2002) suggests, and reason that early and late adaptors of a technology will vary in significant ways, and go on to purposefully sample these operational constructs. The researchers' judgements remain central in identifying these constructs and making judgements based on these to sample information rich cases.

In an apparent move away from the guiding use of judgement before and during investigation, the discussion of the use of confirming and disconfirming cases employs, for the first time, the idea of emergence. Unlike in grounded theory, as discussed in the previous chapter, the concern here is not emergent theory but emergent findings. These can be tested to confirm 'the importance and meaning of possible patterns and checking the viability of emergent findings with new data and additional cases' (2002: 239). Exploratory fieldwork gives way to confirmatory fieldwork in this well ordered account of the research process. Through searching out confirmatory cases researchers can add depth, detail, richness, and credibility to their findings. Through finding disconfirming cases, the researcher is looking for the exceptions that prove the rule. Through these cases, boundaries can be placed around the claims made from the research. Disconfirming cases can help in identifying the limits of what can be said from a piece of research. For Patton there is an important relationship between sampling and research conclusions.

Emergent findings play a part in Patton's next strategy, opportunistic or emergent sampling. In this strategy permitting the sample to emerge during fieldwork is a response to the opportunities that arise in the field. These are unforeseen moments in fieldwork where researchers make on-the-spot decisions to sample something unplanned or change the sampling strategy. Purposeful samples are flexible, led by the data and the judgements made from its interpretation. This strategy accepts that samples cannot be wholly planned in advance in the way that the first eleven strategies in this list are conceived.

The last two sampling strategies return to the theme of a pre-planned sampling strategy, however. The first of these, purposeful random sampling even of small samples will, Patton suggests, substantially increase credibility with certain audiences. Randomisation implies the systemisation of data collection methods, which allows researchers to claim that the cases included in a study were selected without knowing the outcomes of the stories to be told.

For Patton, it is not representativeness but credibility that qualitative researchers are seeking to achieve in a study design. The last of the sampling strategies, sampling politically important cases, is an attempt to design the study in such a way that it grabs the attention of its potential audience. Or, at the least, does not ignite their political sensitivities, leading to the findings from research being quickly undermined. Researchers make strategic and purposeful choices in the design of their studies to 'increase the usefulness and utilization of information where resources permit the study of only a limited number of cases' (Patton, 2002: 241).

As discussed in the last chapter, Morse (2007) uses the term convenience sampling, to describe the early sampling in an objectivist grounded theory approach. Patton (1990; 2002) insists that there is nothing convenient about purposeful sampling. Researchers use these purposeful strategies to carefully select information rich cases. They should avoid convenience sampling, which might be easy, save time, money, and effort, but it yields information-poor cases.

This does not mean that researchers should not be responsive to the unexpected insights that might occur in the research. As this chapter has explained, confirming and disconfirming and opportunistic cases are identified as strategies to test emergent findings and patterns seen in the data. In invoking the idea of opportunism, Patton recognises that researchers must respond through on-the-spot decisions to unexpected encounters in the field. These are careful and thoughtful judgements made during the research. Their purpose is to provide rich, in-depth, and credible cases to support emergent findings and developing conclusions of the research.

Conclusion

Practical concerns in purposeful sampling focus strategic planning to collect information rich cases towards convincing a particular audience. In planning both entry into data collection in the research and accepting that research is done for particular purposes, the 14+1 purposeful sampling strategies incorporate what is known about the phenomena of study and the audiences of the research. Insights gained from both qualitative and quantitative research inform the design of the purposeful sampling strategies in the research.

The focus of purposeful sampling strategies is towards applied research. Dealing with theoretical constructs clearly makes Patton feel a little uneasy. How does one find such things? he seems to be asking. His pragmatic approach to qualitative research takes as read an assumption that the empirical world, suitably examined, provides the findings in qualitative research. Patton characterises the researcher as a practical and strongly reflective decision maker who shapes the research through the judgements made about who or what to purposefully sample.

Patton's pragmatic approach makes the observed unproblematic. He assumes that we learn because we were there, and this should suffice. This follows a long tradition in ethnography. As Clifford Geertz (1988: 1,4) observes:

> 'What a proper ethnographer ought properly to be doing is going out to places, coming back with information about how people live there, and making that information available to the professional community in practical form' ... and further ... 'The ability of anthropologists to get us to take what they say seriously has less to do with either a factual look or an air of conceptual elegance than it has with their capacity to convince us that what they say is a result of their having actually pen- etrated (or, if you prefer, been penetrated by) another form of life, of having, one way or another, truly "been there."'

As a practical account of qualitative research, and sampling in particular, Patton's pragmatic approach is invaluable. This account of sampling in qualitative research turns potential weaknesses into significant strengths. Furthermore, it provides researchers with the insight, and therefore the confidence, to go out and choose who they listen to and what they observe and how to handle the accounts they get in their research. Purposeful sam- pling encourages researchers to use their judgement in making sampling choices. It cuts through epistemological, ontological, and philosophical debates in a refreshing way, while still providing the strategies that allow researchers to learn a great deal about that which we are investigating. But if the pragmatic account of the 14+1 strategies of purposeful sampling has one limitation, it is its unwillingness to engage with the ways in which we bring theory to our research and how we can use theories or ideas strategi- cally to make decisions about who or what to sample in research. We are obliged to return to one of Halcolm's concerns, what do we think is real? It is to a consideration that theories are real, rather than operational con- structs and the implications of this observation for sampling in qualitative research that I consider in the next chapter in an investigation of the case of theoretical or purposive sampling.

3

THEORETICAL OR PURPOSIVE SAMPLING

The third of the three cases embraces theory in a way that neither of the cases discussed so far – theoretical sampling in grounded theory and purposeful sampling – has done. Researchers' intellectual work is pivotal in the progress of the research, which is conceived of as an organic and evolving practice. Both ideas and the empirical contours of the research must be explained in deciding whom or what to sample. Explicitly understanding these processes of engagement are instrumental and strategic in the claims made from research. Theoretical or purposive sampling strategies assume that to explain real phenomena requires more than a faithful abstracted rendering of events and experiences. It requires direct engagement between theory and empirical accounts in an interpretative and inductive strategy of sampling.

The presence of the researcher in the research

Inspired by the events of May 1968 – 'a sudden ray of light on a foggy day ... (that) tore down for a short while the heavy cloak of mass consumption society', Daniel Bertaux and Isabelle Bertaux-Wiame (1981: 171) set out to investigate bread making in France. Their account of the research starts with discussions of their preconceptions and the theoretical framing of the study. This study makes the three domains of ontology, epistemology, and the audience for their research explicit in the research design and its sampling strategies.

Their approach is, they note, 'decidedly structuralist' (1981: 169) in which 'everything should be thought of in terms of relations, not of entities' (1981: 171). These socio-structural relationships between capital and labour are independent of whosoever is occupying that position at the time. What is more, these relationships can be found. The common way of finding these relationships at the time was through statistical investigation. But what if researchers wanted to understand the dynamics of the personal relationships at the heart of these socio-structural relationships? Measured-time variables shorn of context in statistical analysis would be of little value. Knowing these dynamic interpersonal relationships required an experiment with qualitative life-stories; a new way of acquiring evidence and knowledge about these social relationships. Bertaux and Bertaux-Wiame have identified their epistemological position, which was new and met with resistance from other academics. These researchers are strategic. They consider their eventual audience before they start. They discussed with their students and friends who would read their study and concluded that their audience were people who would read books, and those who were 'most remote from the direct confrontation with capital/labour relations' (1981: 172). They set out to find an area to study that was familiar to this audience and decided, after rejecting several options, that the work of making bread would be a productive area of study.

The messiness of getting a sample and the implications of access for framing the possibilities for research is also considered. The Bertaux's plan was to follow the production of bread from wheat field to *boulangerie*, investigating exploitation at each stage in a concrete way. They sought to interview big wheat farmers and mill-owners, but failed to get access. They were more successful accessing farm workers through their union, but the life stories they gave did not tell them about the complex economic transactions involved. The researchers were forced to abandon ideas of asking questions about the life-course of bread making and instead focus their attention on a part of the production of bread, what happened in the artisan bakeries of Paris and, by chance, in the Pyrénées.

Sampling as described by Bertaux and Bertaux-Wiame (1981) is theoretical or purposive. It is directed and re-cast by reflexive researchers towards the purpose of developing and testing theory into an intellectual puzzle about the social world. Made explicit in the planning and execution of the research, including the framing of the sample strategies, are the researchers' understanding of the nature and essence of the social world; what evidence or knowledge is needed to know a social phenomenon; and the audience the researchers want to address with a particular social problem. Furthermore in using theoretical or purposive sampling, researchers do more than act reflectively through engaging in deep and careful thought. They are reflexive. They recognise the presence of researchers in what is being investigated and they actively shape their research in a messy social world, including making ongoing decisions about sampling in their research. Theoretical or purposive sampling is quite different to the approaches to theoretical sampling in grounded theory or the pragmatism of purposeful sampling strategies discussed in the previous two chapters. A theoretical or purposive sampling strategy develops and tests theoretical arguments through strategic sampling strategies chosen to get at what it is the researchers want to know about a universe that they will specify as the research progresses. The claims made from the research are controlled by the many decisions the researchers make, or have forced upon them by the conditions in which they are doing the research. The validity of the research requires researchers to retrace and reconstruct the route through which claims are made. This includes understanding and explaining the sampling done in the research.

Key to theoretical or purposive sampling is recognising that a phenomenon will be revised throughout the research. Research is a process of identifying the conditions under which causal relations operate and then revising explanation based on the investigation of this evidence.

This sampling strategy is explicitly inductive and interpretative (or analytic). For Alfred R. Lindesmith (1968: 13) 'experience is a complex interactional process involving many elements or variables in a series of happenings or events'. Identifying these causal relationships requires 'intensive, exhaustive probing of individual cases and comparison of certain crucial types of cases' (1968: 14). Key to this observation is the emphasis on the decisive and critical nature of choices in the selection of cases. Cases are sampled because they display certain features and their inclusion allows the testing of the explanation being developed in the research. Comparison, as Lindesmith emphasises, is important, but cases may also be chosen because they do not fit with the interpretation and explanation being developed in the research. For Mason (2002) accounting for these negative instances or categories strengthens the explanation of an analytic inductive approach.

Strategic and organic sampling

Indeed, the most exacting descriptions of this induction and interpretation are provided by Jennifer Mason (1996, 2002) who insists that in theoretical or purposive sampling, the process of sampling, data generation and data analysis are viewed and reviewed interactively throughout the research. This approach to sampling advocates the use of quotas, an initial researcher-generated framework to direct sampling from the beginning of the research. These quotas draw on a sampling frame using an interpretative logic rather than one that is representational. Quotas also act as a baseline against which the sampling in the research can be evaluated as it progresses. The key to theoretical or purposive sampling is ensuring that there are opportunities in the research to reflect upon whether quotas are being met and how useful these quotas are proving to be in answering the research questions. Mason (1996: 101) describes this as a stocktaking exercise, the consequence of which may be a modification of an existing sampling quota, or the introduction of a new quota.

In her reworking of theoretical or purposive sampling in a second edition of *Qualitative Researching* (Mason, 2002), a new term is introduced. Theoretical or purposive sampling is described as an organic practice, which grows and develops throughout the research. Sampling in qualitative research, Mason (2002: 127) suggests, is shaped and formed by what the researcher wants to achieve analytically. It is 'crucially related to the emerging shape of the research project'.

The reasons for sampling

The shape of any research project will be guided by the resources available and the purpose of the research. These are the reasons for sampling. Researchers are always faced with the practical problem of a limit on resources. However much we may wish to, everything or everyone cannot be included in a study. There may be unusual circumstances, such as a focussed investigation of a very clearly defined small organisation or collection of documents, where it is conceivable that a whole population could be included in the study, but such studies are likely to be rare. A further practical response to having only limited resources is to try to capture insight, in some way, into a whole population. Mason describes this as a census view. Researchers may make a decision to conduct a broad sweep collection of data. Collecting data from a larger population will always be a trade-off between depth of investigation and breadth. Attempts to collect detailed accounts, which are the common currency of qualitative research, from a large population will, inevitably, lead to further challenges to resources. In designing research there are resource implications to consider not only in collecting data, but also in organising, presenting, and analysing these data. With these considerations in mind, researchers will inevitably choose to focus their study in some way. That is, they will decide on a practical sample with which to carry out an in-depth and detailed study.

It is this requirement for depth of investigation that informs the second reason for sampling. Sampling is done for strategic reasons, because researchers are interested in investigating particular kinds of research questions. Invariably these questions demand the investigation of social phenomena in considerable detail; they are concerned to learn about what, why, and how a social phenomenon happens in a particular natural or real-life setting. As Mason (2002: 121) points out 'qualitative research is very often about depth, nuance and complexity, and understanding how these work'. The focus of sampling in qualitative research is towards achieving a depth of investigation, rather than a breadth of coverage. Researchers seek these in-depth insights to answer their research questions.

Sampling, the research questions, and the claims from the study

Research questions will, of course, vary across the many disciplines of the social sciences, but like the questions pertaining to bread making in Parisian bakeries discussed above, they will be the result of considerable intellectual work that is done in the planning of a study. This early intellectual work is at the heart of how theoretical or purposive sampling is conducted. It allows the researcher to explain to their satisfaction how they understand the nature and

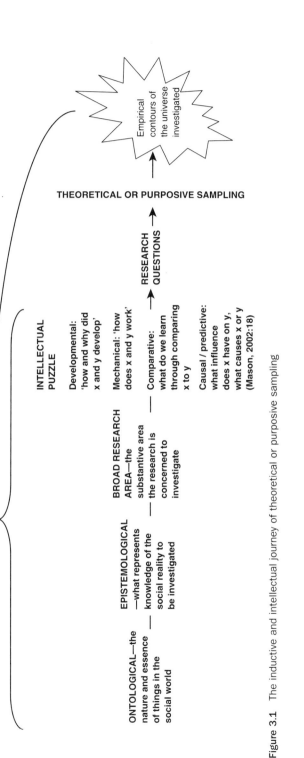

Figure 3.1   The inductive and intellectual journey of theoretical or purposive sampling

essence of the social world they propose to investigate, the evidence or knowledge needed to gain insight into that social world, the broad area of their
research, and the intellectual puzzle that informs their research questions.
Figure 3.1 presents a schematic overview of the path to making decisions
about the sample in theoretical or purposive sampling.

In placing the research question and its foundational intellectual work at the
pivot of her methodology, Mason is mapping out what it means to sample
theoretically or purposively. Theory informs the framing of the study and
therefore the selection of the sample; qualitative researchers make decisions
about who or what to sample from the outset. And furthermore, as research
progresses, theory and this intellectual work continues to direct decisions
about what to purposively sample. As Mason (2002) emphasises in defining
theoretical sampling as:

> selecting groups or categories to study on the basis of their relevance
> to your research question, your theoretical position, your analytic prac-
> tice, and most importantly the argument or explanation that you are
> developing (2002: 124).

This explanation of theoretical or purposive sampling characterises researchers as strongly reflexive. We make decisions, Mason suggests, about how we
see the social world, how this social world can be investigated, and what kinds
of explanations we are concerned to illuminate. These allow us to formulate
research questions in the intellectual work that precedes sampling. Sampling
decisions are acts informed by this intellectual work. In addition, these decisions are driven forward by the empirical and theoretical developments in the
research. A common and misinformed reading of Jennifer Mason's approach
is to assume that the intellectual work is done only at the beginning of the
research. This particular reading concludes that theoretical or purposive sampling merely verifies theory about preconceived universes in the research.
This is not the case. Nor can it be assumed that answers to the ontological
and epistemological questions that frame the intellectual puzzle and research
questions will be perfectly worked through at the beginning of the research.
Mason agrees with the observation made by Clive Seale (1999) that we may
not know our ontological position clearly at the beginning of a piece of
research (Mason, personal communication). Reflexivity, she emphasises,
requires that the intellectual work is revisited throughout the research process
in this inductive strategy.

Setting a baseline for an organic practice of sampling

Researchers start out with a limited understanding of the social phenomenon
they are interested in investigating. As noted, in a theoretical or purposive

sampling strategy considerable intellectual work is done before deciding who or what to sample. The linking of this intellectual work, and its expression in research questions, to sampling is made initially through a sampling quota that seeks to frame the sampling strategy in some way so it relates to this intellectual work. Mason (2002: 128) reminds us that in deciding who or what to sample, reference should always be made to what the research is about and whether those sampled will provide meaningful data to the research. This will help the researcher to 'work out what is the most appropriate unit of classification by which (those sampled) are commonly distinguished'.

This appropriate unit will be a shorthand method of classification. It will describe essential attributes of the sample at the outset. The most common way of doing this is to select characteristics or attributes that are available through common sense or real-life categories. Most often these categories are expressed as variables. These may be variables that are readily available from secondary sources, such as gender, ethnicity, or age, made available from surveys or census data. Alternatively, variables may be characterised by researchers to capture experiences or behaviours.. These variables should, as Mason (2002: 129) emphasises, 'be driven by an interpretative logic which questions and evaluates different ways of classifying (the sample) in the light of the particular concerns of the study'.

The emphasis on interpretative logic is pivotal. Variables will never be adequate to understanding the social processes under investigation. They represent a particular salient attribute of the sample, but they are only an indicator of 'what are essentially complex and differentiated life experiences' (2002: 129). As such, variables are a starting point to locate the sampling quota. To emphasise this point, Mason (2002) contrasts the use of variables in an interpretative logic of qualitative research with the representational logic of stochastic research. This logic, which seeks to make claims to the representativeness of a sample as part of a larger population based on static and cross-sectional variables, is the least commonly used logic of sampling in qualitative research, Mason (2002) contends. A reliance on variables constrains the possibilities for theoretical and analytic advances in the research, whereas, recognising that variables provide a starting point to select a sample with which to investigate fluid, dynamic, and real-life experiences allows researchers to engage critically with these categorical accounts and avoid the dangers of 'slipping into a representational logic' (2002: 131).

As noted, employing a shorthand and critically evaluated account of what may be sampled also supports the development of a quota at the beginning of the research. An example of how a quota might look is presented in Figure 3.2. Here consideration of experience, context, and characteristics describe the sample as meaningfully as possible when the quota is drawn up in the research. This target list also highlights how the sample may well carry

XX sampled, of which

xx will have experienced the phenomenon I'm interested in one way

xx will have experienced the phenomenon I'm interested in another way

xx will have experienced this phenomenon in a particular context

xx will have experience this phenomenon in a different context

xx have this particular characteristic

xx have another particular characteristic

Where XX sampled $\neq \Sigma$xx targets

Figure 3.2 A quota target list

several of the attributes of interest to the research. As can be seen, the final total of the proposed targets is not equal to the sum of each of the sub-targets outlined in the quota target list.

Establishing this quota target guides the selection of the sample from the sampling frame. Mason (2002) goes on to emphasise that 'whatever frame you choose, your sampling practice will thenceforward be influenced by the parameters and characteristics of that frame' (2002: 140–141). In the example of the strategies of theoretical or purposive sampling discussed in the next section, the sampling quota is drawn from a frame which was a survey conducted by the researchers as part of their research.

The strategy of theoretical or purposive sampling

Unlike in survey research, where sampling decisions are made once-and-for-all at the beginning of the project and follows formalised statistical procedures, decisions about theoretical or purposive sampling are made at various stages during the course of fieldwork. These decisions can look rather ad hoc. But, as has been discussed, the application of a theoretical or purposive sampling strategy includes both systematic decision making and flexibility. Janet Finch and Jennifer Mason (1990) describe the ways in which they applied this inductive sampling strategy in a study to investigate family obligation, based upon two different ways of conceptualising obligation: as moral norms structured within society; or as negotiated commitments between individuals.

Their study was divided into two parts. The first part included 978 randomly selected individuals over the age of 18 in the Greater Manchester area of the UK who answered a quantitative survey instrument. In this survey, which had a focus on normative beliefs about family obligations, participants were asked if they were willing to be interviewed as part of a second stage qualitative study; 85% of participants agreed to be re-interviewed. This second stage sought to interrogate 'the complexity of beliefs, as well as the relationship between beliefs and actions, and how people actually negotiate commitments' (1990: 27). This second stage was financially constrained, with 120 interviews budgeted for in the research proposal.

The sampling strategy employed was theoretical, in that the intention was to select the study population on theoretical rather than statistical grounds. According to Finch and Mason (1990: 28), 'theoretical sampling involves a search for the validity of findings rather than representativeness of study populations'. The validity of this theory is dependent upon the quality of the sampling decisions made by researchers in the process of doing the research. This situated theoretical sampling is purposive. In addition to its flexibility and systematic implementation, the approach to sampling is guided by three principles. First, interplay between theory and data collection, reflecting the researchers' concerns that there should always be a close relationship between theory and data collected. Secondly, decisions about who to sample as an ongoing process throughout the research, allowing the researchers to change direction as the research pro-gresses, leaving open the possibility of doing multiple interviews with some respondents and interviewing others individually. Finally, analysis of data and revision of the understanding of the phenomenon as a process that continues throughout the project rather than occurring as a discrete phase, generally after all data is collected.

While this theoretical or purposive sampling is systematic, Finch and Mason (1990) stress that it is inappropriate to lay down a set of general rules. They do insist that decisions made in the research are carefully docu-mented to provide an account of the situated feel of theoretical sampling. A striking feature of the theoretical or purposive sampling strategy pro-posed is the way in which field diaries and research meeting notes are used to systematically describe the sampling decisions made during the research. Drawing extensively on these records, Finch and Mason (1990) highlight three times in the research where theoretical or purposive sampling deci-sions were made, these are the initial sampling decisions; revisiting sampling decisions during the fieldwork; and on-going strategies of taking stock of fieldwork.

Initial sampling decisions

At the beginning of the research, the researchers considered whom to select from the survey, with this selection acting as the sampling frame for their study. In making these decisions they wanted to retain opportunities for flexibility to select further respondents, particularly to move beyond the individuals who had responded to the survey instrument. Field notes from an early planning meeting highlight the following decisions:

- A focus on the research problem using a sampling quota of two sub-groups of five divorced and five recently remarried women under the age of 25 years using the survey as the sampling frame developed in the first phase of the research. This relatively small sample would allow for further individuals to be chosen later within the resource constraints of the research.
- A decision to start with interviewing women only and then decide if it was useful to employ a male researcher to interview male participants.
- Select women to the two sub-groups randomly, rather than selecting women to many sub-groups based on the experiences expressed in the survey results. The researchers theorised that it was likely that the two sub-groups they chose to sample were 'likely to have undergone some renegotiation, which would make issues of obligation explicit' (1990: 31) and were likely to have experienced significant social changes in their family relationships.
- There was a discussion about whether to include a control group, but this was rejected because the aim of the research was not to generalise from a representative sample, but to allow for further sample selection driven by an inductive and interpretative logic.

These key decisions highlight four features of the theoretical or purposive sample. First, the stress is on depth over breadth of coverage. The researchers decided on a quota target of a relatively small number of individuals from only two sub-groups. The emphasis is on gaining detailed, rich accounts from participants, which provide insight that can inform further theoretical or purposive sampling.

Secondly, theoretical significance guides the sampling decisions. The researchers bring their experience to bear, recognising that in choosing these particular sub-groups they are most likely to gain insight into the negotiation and renegotiation of family relationships they are seeking to investigate. Furthermore, the ontological position of the researchers is made clear in their sampling strategy. This is expressed in their recognition of the inadequacy of the frame they are using, the sample survey they have collected and analysed.

Thirdly, this initial stage of selection through random selection from the sampling frame sought not to prejudge findings. The only limits placed on selection were the age of participant and whether they were divorced or recently remarried. The researchers had concerns about the potential diversity of their sample, along dimensions of class, ethnicity, and employment status for instance. But they decided not to include these selection criteria at this initial stage of sampling. Instead, they proposed that they would select respondents for their sample along these dimensions and others if they felt it was appropriate. This approach, Finch and Mason (1990: 34) observe 'left open the possibility of rethinking the strategy at a later stage'. The emphasis at this early stage in theoretical or purposive sampling is to be both systematic and flexible.

Finally, the researchers are concerned to balance the aims of the study against the resources available to conduct research. The decisions made in this initial stage of sampling leave open opportunities to plan future sampling strategies. A decision about whether to recruit men to the research, and therefore employ a male researcher, was postponed until insight had been gained from the initial sample. Similarly, decisions about the selection of kin to the study were only made once the initial sampling and data collection were underway.

Revisiting sampling decisions during the fieldwork

The intention of the family obligation study was to interview participants selected from the sampling frame and then conduct follow up interviews with their relatives about the same experiences of family negotiations. This second stage of the sampling selection had the purpose of identifying strategies to recruit these kin to the research. The researchers therefore had to make decisions about whose relatives should be interviewed and how they would define the kin group to be followed up. Initial decisions about these selection criteria were made at an early stage of the study in a planning meeting just one-and-a-half months after the initial sampling strategy had been decided. In this planning meeting the researchers decided:

- To treat the respondent who answered the survey instrument and had agreed to be interviewed in the qualitative research as the central person in the kin group. This would mean that kin were directly related in some way to respondents in the initial sample. This strategy would avoid a haphazard sample being selected.
- The criteria for inclusion were that the relative was significant from the respondent's point of view. The researchers had been told in the interview by the respondent that the relative had been directly involved in some way in negotiations of family obligations. Relatives who had been involved in the past but were not now in contact with the respondent were excluded. So too were relatives who had been involved in a crisis situation; the researchers considered their inclusion in the research might raise ethical concerns.
- The selection of kin groups for intensive study were those in which the initial respondent had described how kin had offered financial and material support.

These decisions emphasise the relationships between sampling decisions and resources in directing strategies in theoretical or purposive sampling. The role researchers' play in reflexively engaging with intellectual work throughout the research process is emphasised too. Decisions about how social phenomena such as the nature of kin groups, what constitutes a significant relative, and what constitutes support, and methodological decisions about how far along a kinship network to carry on recruiting and interviewing are each framed and defined by the researchers. These decisions will have implications for the claims to be made from the study about the universe represented. Throughout their meeting-notes, research-notes, and commentary are evaluations of how a balance is achieved between 'getting very detailed information from a very small number of kin groups, and including a range of different experiences in the study' (Finch and Mason, 1990: 37). In an ideal world with infinite resources one would seek both depth of account and breadth of coverage. Resources always mediate these decisions, as do ethical considerations. The theoretical or purposive sampling strategy outlined here obliges the researchers to keep making decisions to curtail their sampling strategy, despite knowing that further interesting insight might emerge for the research. Researchers have to be 'prepared to sacrifice ... possibilities in order to create a systematic selection strategy' (1990: 37). Other researchers, Finch and Mason remind us, might well take rather different decisions.

Taking stock of the fieldwork and moving on: ongoing sampling decisions

Taking stock in a theoretical and purposive sampling strategy seeks to assess and modify the sampling strategy during the research. It is fine-tuning and, at the same time, an opportunity to reflect on how data help to modify theory. This strategy, informed by an analytic inductive approach, seeks to test and revise theory through theoretical or purposive sampling strategies that select and compare certain crucial types of cases.

A stocktaking exercise may happen at any stage during the research and it may be repeated. Janet Finch and Jennifer Mason conducted a first stocktaking exercise about four months after the initial planning meeting. At this time 41 interviews were completed and 17 firmly arranged of a proposed target of 120 interviews. Their deliberations were based on a discussion document prepared by Janet Finch. The key issues addressed in this exercise described in meeting notes were:

- Identifying and addressing groups the researchers expected to be included in the sample but who were not adequately represented. These groups included men, who had been excluded from the research in the initial planning meeting because the researchers did not have the resources to interview them. In the stocktaking exercise the researchers identified the importance of their inclusion. Strategies to ensure the researchers' safety while carrying out interviews with this part of their sample were discussed.

- The researchers considered that unemployment was an important contemporary issue. They also felt that unemployment had implications for their work. The sampling frame provided data on employment status, but this was now one year old. They decided to approach respondents who had been unemployed at the time of the survey, but to exclude older unemployed people.
- The third underrepresented group in the sample were people from ethnic minority groups. In discussing how to involve these groups, decisions were made about how these groups could be included and whether the question structure of the interview schedule was appropriate. Individual records from the survey were read before individuals were approached.
- The researchers also noted a bunching of respondents in middle class social groups, living in owner-occupied housing. A decision was made to make a particular effort to recruit respondents from the highest social class and from the manual social classes. This was done for theoretical reasons. Janet Finch noted that their data suggested continuing friendship after divorce between ex-partners in the middle class group and wondered if this was particular to this group.
- The researchers confirmed their focus in the research on divorce and widowhood, especially for those less than 50 years old, which they reasoned would have similar experiences to divorced respondents. They decided to follow up on divorced or widowed individuals from kin groups.
- They reaffirmed their criteria for the selection of respondents, in particular ensuring that fit elderly people be recruited to the study. They were concerned to ensure these respondents were not involved in crisis situations, which they had considered in the initial meeting to be an ethically difficult area to research.
- They prioritised the inclusion of step-parents, because this was a central issue in the research. The researchers agreed to review the questionnaires from the survey and identify step-parents for inclusion in the study from the kin groups.
- Once again the researchers made decisions about how many respondents to sample, based on the data they already had, the resources available to them, and their discussions in the stocktaking exercise. Again the numbers were small, ten men, of whom five would be divorced/remarried and five young adults. They also sought to intersect other categories in this quota, so hoped to recruit male respondents who were in lower and higher social classes, for example.
- They agreed to hold another stocktaking exercise later in the research to assess how well the categories they had identified were represented.

This stocktaking exercise supported the adjustment of the sample. Finch and Mason observe how, at a stage in the research, they felt confident about the ideas/theories being generated from the intellectual work that linked theoretical developments in the research with data through sampling and analysis. This is an analytic inductive strategy, which, according to Znaniecki:

has been called the *type* method or method of *typical cases*. ... type originally meant a mould, a pattern after which a multiplicity or individual instances were shaped and thus akin to the "*eidos*" or "idea" in a Platonic sense, as prefiguring a class of real data (1934: 251: emphasis in the original).

The metaphor of the mould employed by Znaniecki provides a useful visual image of the way in which analytic induction is conceptualised. Derived from Platonic philosophy, the idea, as εἶδος (eidos), form, or type, is the perfect representation from which imperfect copies or approximations are made. Perfect abstract patterns as theories are brought into engagement with the contours of empirical data. Janet Finch's observation about friendship after divorce provides an example of analytic induction being applied. The researchers had a theory, which they called the 'Posy Simmonds effect'. This theory was informed by the specific instances from the research, the empirical contours of the data they had collected. It also drew on their theoretical expertise.

Posy Simmonds is a British cartoonist whose middle class characters always seem to get on after divorce. She publishes many of her cartoons in a liberal daily broadsheet newspaper. Theoretical insight, rather nicely summarised using Posy Simmonds' images, are brought into engagement with empirical data in the research. In describing the phenomenon as the 'Posy Simmonds effect' the researchers are developing an abstract type, which resonates through the theoretical or purposive decisions of sampling. The real is not discovered, emergent, or constructed from empirical data, this analytic induction suggests. It is, as Mason (1996, 2002) emphasises, based in the ongoing intellectual work through the research. Theoretical or purposive sampling respects the contours of empirical investigation, always informed by the research question, theoretical position, analytic practice, and the argument or explanation developed throughout the research. Cases, as typical, comparative, or negative for instance, are moulded by both ideas and empirical data. They are selected in the research to allow for the reasoning of theoretical statements of general relevance (Greenhalgh et al., 2011).

In addition, arriving at the typical in the research allows Finch and Mason (1990) to observe that they felt they were in less danger of losing their focus than they had been at the beginning of the research in their decisions about who to sample. This is reflected in the fine tuning and filling in of types evident in this stocktaking exercise. These decisions are made for two reasons. First, decisions can be made to sample groups where extra resources and effort are needed. In this stocktaking exercise, men, upper class groups, and ethnic minority groups were identified as hard-to-reach, for example.

The second set of decisions extends the particular instances under investigation and the claims that can be made from the research. The decision to purposively recruit unemployed people, for instance, extends the scope of the research questions being asked and therefore the inferences made from the investigation. The emphasis in the account of these decisions was that it was a 'contemporary issue' (1990: 44). The research was conducted between 1985 and 1989. Unemployment in the UK peaked in 1986 at just over 10% of the labour force. The latest unemployment figures featured regularly in news bulletins. It was a feature of popular consciousness. Sampling people who were unemployed at the time of the survey was justified in the research for this reason and incorporated into the typical cases of the research.

An account of the sample in the research is developed through doing the research and through the many decisions that informed the research and were shaped through the experience of collecting data. Early quota samples are established based on the intellectual work that preceded the research. New decisions are made in relation to what is learnt through the ongoing research. A discussion of what constitutes a good informant emphasises this point. Mason observes that she is worried that she will only follow up good informants, by whom she means those who are articulate and talk directly to the issues in the research in an analytic way. These informants reflect and philosophise on the instances and processes being studied. Other informants, Mason notes, talk about similar instances and processes but do not make them sound as inherently fascinating. She expresses what she describes as a 'nagging doubt' that the she might systematically exclude from the study those she feels are less interesting. Finch responds to this reflective account of fieldwork with her own considerations of the ways in which she found listening to the tapes of those that Mason found less satisfying. She observes that she found interesting issues to pursue, but did not feel influenced by the nature of the interaction. The importance of the team in making decisions about who to sample are reinforced. The focus of sampling strategies is on identifying best cases to provide insight into the research questions.

These repeated decisions throughout the research are systematic. Researchers are highly visible in all the decisions about who to sample in the research. They are not led by emerging theory from the empirical data, but by the empirical contours of specific instances in the research and their own explicit theorisation before, during, and after the fieldwork. Their detailed field notes and meeting notes are intended to capture 'the changing contexts of (sampling) decisions, their purposes and consequences, and the principles underlying them' (Finch and Mason, 1990: 49). Theoretical or purposive sampling strategies are an expression of these decisions. The careful recording of the many decisions made in the research and how these led to identifying crucial types of cases allows for judgements to be made about the universe that is being sampled in the research.

Defining a universe: an emerging interpretative account of the sample

Researchers invariably seek a wider resonance for their research through either empirical or theoretical generalisability. Mason (2002: 195) recognises that any generalisation is 'grounded in the empirical contours of your project'. As the previous section has considered, these contours are mapped between the coordinates of decisions made about whom or what to sample in the research and the specific instances that are sampled. Theoretical or purposive sampling strategies allow researchers to say something meaningful about what the chosen sample signifies or encapsulates. In other words, the empirical and theoretical universe or population the sample represents. By linking the decisions about whom or what to sample both empirical and theoretical considerations are combined and claims can be made about how the chosen sample relates to a wider universe or population.

As noted from Finch and Mason's (1990) account of theoretical or purposive sampling discussed above, other universes or populations than the one chosen can always be selected. There must be a direct link between sampling strategy and a clear articulation of the universe represented.

There are also safeguards inherent in this methodological strategy to ensure that decisions about what is sampled are not driven forward merely by the personal preferences of the researcher. The research question and intellectual puzzle capture the researchers' understandings of the social phenomena being investigated and the way in which we can legitimately generate knowledge. As Norman Blaikie (2010) observes, these ontological and epistemological assumptions in research strategies are not independent of each other. The research design and the choices about whom or what to sample must be shown to map coherently onto the theoretical assumptions in the research, in one direction, and theoretically and empirically onto the universe as described by the researchers in the other direction.

The ability to describe the universe from which a sample has been drawn is, therefore, fundamental to the rigour of claims made from theoretical or purposive sampling. Qualitative research, as has been emphasised, cannot follow the representative logic of stochastic research, in which claims can be made with a degree of confidence that findings are representative of a larger population. In using this interpretative and inductive strategy, Mason (2002) points out that the significance of sampling categories is defined in both theoretical and empirical terms; even so, the claims from this strategy are theoretical. Mason suggests five different kinds of theoretical generalisation:

First, researchers may claim that the findings from a study are typical of a population or universe in some way. This claim does not stem from sampling strategies that seek a representative sample so the claims that can be made are rather weak. Claims may be made, however, that there is little reason to suspect the sample to be atypical using some identified characteristic.

Secondly, through detailed sampling of a social process in a particular setting, it may be possible to gain insights into the ways in which a similar process might happen in other settings. Claims can be made into what might be possible based on observations that 'these seemed to be the key explanatory factors and elements in the process in the setting' (Mason, 2002: 196). These insights can then lead the researcher to identify potential lessons for other settings, invariably posed as questions to be asked about whether these lessons have a wider resonance in these other settings.

Thirdly, researchers may purposively sample extreme, unusual, or pivotal issues or processes with reference to a particular theory to explore how the phenomena being investigated aid in developing or extending a body of that theory.

Fourthly, in choosing a sample, researchers may select issues or processes that have the potential to provide strategic comparisons, which 'enable the testing and developing of theoretical and explanatory propositions'. These may be 'key dimensions of the intellectual puzzle or interesting possibilities' (Mason, 2002: 196).

Finally, researchers may show how and why particular issues or processes work in particular contexts, where these contexts have been strategically selected. This approach allows for potential cross-contextual generalisations to be made, which demonstrates how context and explanation are intimately connected through using specificity and difference in the sampled issues or processes.

These five ways of understanding theoretical generalisation point to strategies for sampling in theoretical or purposive sampling. In deciding what is typical or something that happens in a particular setting, research can provide illustrative and evocative accounts. The emphasis in making these decisions for sampling is to understand these strategies as underpinned by an interpretative logic. This logic, as has been emphasised, is characterised by in-depth investigation, which seeks insight that is a nuanced, close-up, and meticulous account of the social processes or phenomenon under investigation. Using this detailed approach does not mean abandoning rigour in the research, however. Nor, as the earlier discussion has emphasised, does it mean that this inductive strategy is only concerned with investigating the particular. Researchers must make decisions about whom or what to sample, and be able to describe:

> a relationship where the sample is designed to encapsulate a *relevant range* of units in relation to the wider universe, but not to represent it directly. (Mason, 1996: 92).

These observations about sampling logic leave open the question of what kind of relationship exists between the sample and wider population. As Mason (2002) observes, this will not be a straightforward representation. Special or pivotal units may have significance in the research. They will be significant theoretically, because they will enable researchers to test and develop theoretical propositions. Relationships between context and phenomena will also be important. And, as has already been emphasised, there should be a direct link between the decisions made in sampling, data analysis, and the types of social explanation they intend to develop. This iteration, Mason (2002) argues, influences sampling conceptually and procedurally.

Theoretical or purposive sampling, therefore, is not merely a matter of improvisation, accident, or arbitrary choice. Decisions are made that justify the sample, because it does work in the research. It allows for certain kinds of analysis to be done because the sample depicts, portrays, or symbolises a particular universe that the researcher can describe. Theoretical or purposive sampling is never ad hoc or unspecified, even though it is often not possible to calculate the degree to which a sample represents its wider universe. Ad hoc sampling is undesirable because it severely limits analytic possibilities in the study. Blaikie (2010: 177) goes further, describing this sampling as lazy and naïve and the 'most extreme and unsatisfactory form of non-probability sampling'.

Nor, as can be seen, is this theoretical or purposive sampling synonymous with theoretical sampling as described in grounded theory. The key differences lie in the role of researchers as decision makers; how they conceptualise, mobilise, and refine theory in the research process, and how relationships between theory, critical, typical, or unique cases, and empirical observations from these cases are mobilised towards an analysis, and the claims made from research. Placing researcher reflexivity at the heart of the sampling strategy emphasises the strategic role researchers play in deciding who or what to sample in the research. Choosing crucial types of cases in the analytic inductive approach of theoretical or purposive sampling justifies the generalisations that can be made from the research. The universe as identified through the research is a closed system, the sampling of cases is antecedent to its identification.

Conclusion

In theoretical or purposive sampling strategies researchers have to do considerable intellectual work in deciding and justifying their strategy of sampling, because the sample has to do a great deal of work in the study. Decisions about whom or what to sample must be shown to relate to an understanding of the social world being investigated and the kinds of explanation the researchers are seeking to answer from the study. At the same time these decisions must be responsive to empirical observation and theoretical development within the research. Researchers must also be able to give an account of how the sample signifies or relates to a particular universe. Crucial to this organic sampling practice are the ways in which it supports theoretical generalisation and the evocative and illustrative accounts from the research. In seeking to undertake a particular kind of analysis researchers shape and form their sample reflexively.

This account of theoretical and purposive sampling characterises researchers as making sampling decisions in the research from the very earliest stages of planning a study through to its completion. It recognises that all research is faced with resource and ethical constraints. The role of researchers in shaping the research they do through the ways in which they frame their study and make decisions about the sampling strategy are central to this approach. The emphasis here is not on a reflective responsiveness to the unfolding empirical findings in a study, but researchers as reflexive agents who make decisions about who or what to sample and the universe this relates to.

This investigation of theoretical or purposive sampling shows that interpretative and inductive strategies bring social theory to research, and how researchers repeatedly decide throughout their research what to study, with whom, and when. Theoretical or purposive sampling strategies are part of a methodological strategy of defining cases in the research so as to make claims for their investigation. These claims are invariably theoretical and go beyond the propinquity of their empirical investigation.

Michael Quinn Patton, whose practical and pragmatic strategy of purposeful sampling was described in the last chapter, boldly asserts, without feeling any need for referencing, that qualitative research is mature enough to be accepted as a legitimate method for understanding the social world. It can provide valuable insights. It does not need to abide by rules of objectivity derived from a positivist world view and so carefully developed by Glaser and Strauss (1967) and repeated by Glaser (1992) in their account of theoretical sampling.

Moreover, objectivity is not a fixed social and scientific phenomenon to be achieved through a methodological twist in the research. It has, according to Lorraine Daston and Peter Galison (2007), changed in definition since first flipping its meaning with subjectivity in the seventeenth century. Objectivity in scientific representation has undergone three distinct phases of definition in modern times. In the seventeenth and eighteenth centuries objectivity was defined with reference to the presentation of the perfect God-like representation. More recently, in the nineteenth and into the mid-twentieth century, objectivity was evaluated with reference to the materially observed, assiduously accurate presentation of fact. This is the mechanical objectivity which underpins the theoretical sampling strategies of early grounded theory. More recently, Daston and Galison (2007) acknowledge a new representation of objectivity, as informed judgement. This account embraces the expertise of scientists in their interpretation of the objects they investigate, be these the medical world of the anatomical atlas, or the investigation and theorising of social phenomena by social scientists.

Theoretical or purposive sampling strategies discussed in this chapter give central importance to recognising the ways in which researchers apply their trained judgement and make decisions in their empirical investigation.

As was discussed in Chapter 1, constructivist grounded theorists have increasingly recognised the ways in which social researchers bring theory to their research and therefore, in some way, shape the theoretical sample. In accounting for what is perceived to be a reflexive turn, this constructivism remains agnostic about these theories. Agnosticism holds that the existence of anything beyond and behind material phenomena is unknown. It is assumed that the real can be directly perceived and described and the outcome of the research is a construed described empiricism.

Accounts of theoretical or purposive sampling take a quite different approach. Critical cases are selected through theoretical (or intellectual) work that both informs and holds fast to the empirical contours of the social phenomena being investigated. Agnosticism is replaced by a belief in theory, as sets of ideas that can be interpreted through qualitative researching. The analytic induction of theoretical or purposive sampling strategies assumes that to interpret phenomena and generalise about these requires more than a faithful abstracted rendering of events and experiences. It requires direct engagement between theory and empirical accounts. Sampling is the strategy, organically developed in the research through which perfect abstract patterns are brought into play with empirical evidence to select cases, be these typical, negative instances, or used to promote comparison in the research. Theoretical or purposive sampling strategies outlined and developed in two editions of *Qualitative Researching* (Mason, 1996, 2002) provide a detailed and considered account of the implications of an analytic and strongly interpretative methodology to sampling in qualitative research.

These continue a methodological tradition of analytic induction in qualitative research that can be traced back to the philosophical writings of Znaniecki (1934), who observed that insight into the social world proceeds through constituting logical classes of things. Such constitutions are not possible from 'pure empirical reality' (1934: 252) but are defined through both intellectual work and the empirical contours of the case. Analytic induction, the acts of moving from specific case to a general theory and back to another case, is made possible through cases, made up as they are of packages of data and theory to be transferred from one particular instance to other particular instances.

For a realist sampling strategy there is a limitation to this approach to sampling in qualitative research. Theoretical or purposive sampling, with its strategies of induction and interpretation, relies on the incorporation of atomistic events enveloped in a closed system of the researchers' intellectual work to produce critical, typical, or unique cases. Now, as outlined in Proposition One of the Introduction, social reality is not simply captured through interpretation and ideas but is richer and deeper. A realist sampling strategy must explain the causal powers, liabilities, and dispositions inherent in a complex, open and stratified social, natural, and physical system. Addressing these challenges are the focus of the second part of this book.

PART TWO
CHOOSING CASES

4

THE BASICS OF REALIST SAMPLING

This chapter elaborates an account of scientific realism, through developing the five propositions for realism discussed in the introduction of this book. It goes on to consider the implications of these observations on doing realist research. The focus of this chapter and rest of the book is on choosing cases in scientific realist qualitative research. In this chapter the ways in which presuppositions that express the interplay of human agency and structures and their causal powers in complex systems are implicated in research is discussed. The quest of realist research is good interpretation and explanation. Sampling in both qualitative and quantitative research, and across the natural sciences, social sciences, comparative research, and historical investigation can be thought of as cases. Research draws together bundles of real ingredients that have quite different forms and functions. One chooses the bundle best suited to test a theory of how that which is being investigated can be explained. The trick in choosing cases is to assemble the optimal configuration of ingredients to refine a theory and then to repeat the trick within the resource constraints of the research project. Within any research it is theories that inform the choice of sample, and the sampling strategies that are used to test theory. At the outset, these theories are not the result of sense data (empiricism). They are guesses held up as bold conjectures which always refer to real phenomena. The chapter starts with a historical example of these processes happening in research and builds on the lessons from this case to elaborate the key dimensions of a realist sampling strategy.

The relationship between theory and evidence in research: the case of cholera in 1854

In the late summer of 1854 there was an outbreak of Asiatic cholera in Golden Square, a district of Soho, London. It killed 616 people. This epidemic and the science of its interpretation have produced an enduring myth, which will be familiar to geographers, epidemiologists, and public health specialists. At the heart of this legend is the relationship between empirical evidence and theory. The often repeated story holds that Dr John Snow, a public health physician and early pioneer of anaesthesia, drew a map of the households in which people had died from cholera, applied an early and innovative version of network analysis, and established that the source of the epidemic was a hand pump in Broad Street. He ordered the removal of the pump handle and mortality from the epidemic declined rapidly. More heroic accounts have him removing the hand pump himself. The way in which Dr John Snow and other investigators proceeded to understand this outbreak and attribute cause is rather different however.

Snow had a theory, which at the time was held by only a minority of public health physicians. He believed that cholera was caused by a 'morbid material', most likely carried in water that, when drunk, caused cholera. A year after the cholera epidemic in Golden Square had abated Snow published considerable evidence to support his theory (Snow, 1855), which included a natural epidemiological study, case studies collected from cholera epidemics across Britain, and the famous map of cholera deaths around the Broad Street Pump. This map, which he did not actually draw until three months after the epidemic and subsequently revised, was used to test a hypothesis, derived from a theory about the cause of cholera.

John Snow was not the only map maker busy tracking cholera deaths in Golden Square. An engineer for the Metropolitan Commission of Sewers, Edmund Cooper, also set to work to evince the cause of the cholera outbreak. His map, which was more detailed than Snow's, was used to test a quite different theory. He argued that, to use Snow's words, 'cholera depends on an unknown something in the atmosphere which becomes localized, and has its effects increased by the gases given off from decomposing animal and vegetable matters.' (Snow, 1855). This miasmatist theory of disease transmission was the dominant theory of the time. Cooper's employers were particularly concerned that he should find evidence to prove it was not their sewers that were the cause of the cholera outbreak. This Cooper managed to do successfully through showing that there was no relationship between the households where deaths had been experienced and the route of the sewer through Golden Square. His interpretation was, like John Snow's, a result of the clash of preconceived theory and empirical data. Cooper's interpretation held sway with the Committee on Scientific Inquiries of the General Board of Health too. They rejected Snow's account that relied on a theory of water borne disease, preferring instead to attribute the cholera epidemic to putrefying organic matter. It would be some time before the fallible miasmatist theory of disease was finally laid to rest and replaced with another theory, with which many will be familiar, the Germ Theory. Our understanding of everything from the design of hospital wards, through public health advice on procedures for washing our hands in a flu epidemic, to the ways in which populations respond to epidemics of infectious disease are informed by the theory John Snow was testing. This theory is the dominant idea about the causative agents of infection. It informs medical and public health practice and research. It remains provisional and constantly open to revision, however. It is a theory and is generally held to be the closest approximation to reality, at least for the moment.

Ideas and evidence

The myth-making of John Snow's mapping research exemplifies a dualism that has informed much of modern science method in one way or another. The mind and the physical world are separate, independent, and irreducible entities. They have nothing in common. The legend holds that it is empirical data that led to a theory of how cholera spread. This has John Snow simply seduced into making associations between empirical points on a map as the variable of cholera deaths, and their proximity to a water pump, as Howard Brody and colleagues (2000) suggest.

But while John Snow and Edmund Cooper came at the problem they were researching with quite different ideas, their approach was realist. Each of them assumed not a dualism between empirical research and theory, but that their ideas and the evidence in the research were interacting parts of a single world. The concepts and meanings they brought to their research were as real as the records they mapped to the slum houses along the roads upon which the unfortunate victims of cholera lived. As Joseph Maxwell (2012: 18) observes, for realist researchers:

> Concepts, meanings and intentions are as real as rocks; they are just not as accessible to direct observation and description as rocks. In this way they are like quarks, black holes, the meteor impact that supposedly killed the dinosaurs, or William Shakespeare: we have no way of directly observing them, and our claims about them are based on a variety of sorts of indirect evidence.

The central contention of this chapter is that researchers bring ideas, preconceptions, concepts, meanings, and intentions to their research. A shorthand way of describing these mental activities is to call this real intellectual work theory. This theory cannot be divorced from the institutions within which we do research and for whom we do research. It frames the research we conduct through the language and concepts we use to describe the attributes of the people, organisations, books, images, webpages, or whatever we choose to research. For a realist there is a relationship between mental processes and that which is directly observable and recordable. Both must be accounted for in any description of the research we do. By extension, sampling in realist qualitative research works out the relation between theory and evidence of the samples we select. This chapter investigates the implications of this relationship. But before exploring the implications of realism to sampling in qualitative research in detail, the next section frames realism as scientific realism. Scientific realism is one of very many versions of realism applied across the sciences.

Scientific realism

The scientific realist account of sampling (invariably contracted to realist sampling) developed in the rest of this book draws on and is influenced by insights that may be traced to the critical realism of Roy Bhaskar (1979) and Margaret Archer (1998). Realism contends that there is an underlying reality independent of our ability to see, measure, or even know what is happening. As Bhaskar (2008: 250) concludes in his investigation of a realist theory of science:

> Things exist and act independently of our descriptions, but we can only know them under particular descriptions. Descriptions belong to the world of society and of men ... Science, then, is the systematic attempt to express in thought the structures and ways of action of things that exist and act independently of thought.

There is a world without humans, but there can never be knowledge without the powers that go before the creation of knowing. In considering these powers Andrew Sayer's (1992, 2000) investigation of a realist natural and social science and his focus on the ways in which objects and social relations have causal powers contributes to this discussion. So too, recent accounts that have tackled the practical implications of a realism (Danermark et al., 1997) in qualitative research. But the central realist postulate that within any research, including a piece of qualitative research investigating the social world, real internal mechanisms can be manipulated and acted upon to produce particular outcomes in an open social system (Bhaskar, 1979), remains remarkably intransigent to practical methodological accounts. There are exceptions, and these are the outlines of scientific realism, described by Ray Pawson and Nick Tilley (1997) and Ray Pawson (2006, 2013) and a more plural realist account of realist qualitative research (Maxwell, 2012). These authors draw on a similar heritage to my own, in denying

> that we can have any 'objective' or certain knowledge of the world, and accept the possibility of alternative valid accounts of any phenomenon. All theories about the world are seen as grounded in a particular perspective and world view, and all knowledge is partial, incomplete, and fallible. (Maxwell, 2012: 12 – emphasis in the original)

In a similar way, the sample in qualitative research cannot be defined objectively, and described in its entirety through its objects, properties, and relations. Realists may assume that the sample is the way it is, while recognising that it is a conceptual scheme, interpretative, explanatory, and provisional.

A realist sampling strategy and the concomitant acts of casing are social objects. They have historical antecedence, however short the time period, which links the choices made to events that precede them. These horizontal explanations require '*vertical* explanations in terms of the generative relationships indispensable for their realisation' (Archer, 1998: 196 – emphasis in the original). For Roy Bhaskar (1998: 25 – emphasis in the original) 'social forms are a necessary condition of any intentional act' like sampling and choosing cases. The pre-existence of these acts of choosing cases 'establishes their *autonomy* as possible objects of scientific investigation and that their *causal power* establishes their *reality*'. The purpose of this part of the book is to investigate the vertical liabilities and dispositions that are internal and external to the research, that express their causal powers on the horizontal regularity of the intentional acts of a realist sampling strategy and its outcome.

Describing a realist sample

The realist sample may be described as an empirical fact, but at the same time it is necessary to explain the powers of a particular sample in the research. Realists insist on stratified reality and causal powers. Generative mechanisms, as powers and liabilities, act between experiences and events for their regularity to happen. Sayer (2000) suggests that most often in social science research we are concerned to understand two ontological strata. The domains of the empirical and actual are considered together, thus allowing for observation of factual events and how these are experienced. The second domain is that of the real. This is the domain where mechanisms or emergent powers have the potential to trigger events. A further way of considering this stratification is to accept that dynamic and complex social reality is characterised by the interdependencies of agency and structure. Agency can be seen and recorded from empirical and actual events and experiences. There are, however, real generative mechanisms that govern, mediate, and facilitate these events and experiences. Sampling in qualitative research is stratified in a similar way.

A realist description of sampling in qualitative research will consider what happens in the acts of sampling that impact on the potential claims from the research. Here, scientific realism is useful because its methodology expressly recognises that the causal relationships that bring about particular social phenomena can be disclosed, made visible, and, to a degree explained. It is this potential to articulate the mechanisms that inform choices in the acts of sampling carried out in research that is of concern. The assumptions that brought about sampling choices can be disclosed and, in doing so, stronger claims to understanding the sample can be made.

Sampling will always be a construction of something. We may, for instance, choose a sample of men, women, children of a certain age, these documents, web pages, visual images in an archive, or whatever because they will best provide insight into the social phenomenon to be investigated. This describes the sample, using Sayer's schema, in the domains of the empirical and actual, expressed as observable categories and variables. This domain is most amenable to our interpretation and features most often in accounts of the samples we use in research. It does not explain the real sample, only its empirical features.

To characterise the sample more adequately the social powers that govern, mediate, and facilitate the choices of the empirical sample to be studied in the research must be disclosed. These social powers produce the sample. For realists, these are generative mechanisms.

Some of these generative mechanisms are beyond the control of researchers, they are external and contingent, but must, nonetheless, be explained if we are to understand the sample in the research. Others, the internal powers, are the theories, models, and concepts researchers bring to the research. These are social constructions, but of a relatively weak kind. Throughout the research we will make rational, yet fallible judgements about the competing theories, models, and concepts that frame the sample (Olsen, 2004).

The description of the sample will change throughout the research as evidence and ideas are worked out. The generative mechanisms that govern the sample are dynamic, and changeable. Ideas are refined and developed as the research progresses. Someone or something may be chosen to be included in the study at the outset for a particular theoretical reason. But as the research progresses, the set of ideas as to why that unit is included in the study will be refined through the interaction and insight gained in the study.

A description of sampling requires an account of these generative mechanisms, the internal and external powers that frame choices. The empirical and actual domains of this model of realist sampling will be familiar to all researchers. These are the categorical accounts of events and experiences, common in most reports from qualitative research, that describe a sample. The linguistic fallacy inherent in this description is addressed shortly, but before addressing this, I consider the domain of the real – the generative mechanisms as powers and liabilities that frame choices in realist qualitative research.

Generative mechanisms in sampling

For realists, generative mechanisms govern, mediate, impede, and facilitate sampling choices. These are the powers that describe sampling. The ways in which these causal powers are implicated in explanations and the ways in which they differ from events and experiences are often explained by realists through considering the capacity of gunpowder to explode. In part, this is accounted for through its chemical composition of potassium nitrate, charcoal, and sulphur. But, as Sayer (1981) reminds us, it only has this capacity to produce an exothermic reaction and a loud bang if certain powers are applied to the gunpowder. To explode it needs the right kind of spark, under the right atmospheric conditions; it must be packed to the correct density, and so on. But it needs more than just the right chemical and physical conditions – social conditions are needed too. To use a parochial example, which will be more familiar to readers in England: if, as happened on the night of the 5th November 1605, Guy Fawkes with matches and touchwood in his pocket and gunpowder ready and primed, was arrested, then the gunpowder's potential to explode and blow up the British House of Lords will not be realised. Gunpowder has the determined capacity to explode, but this is not pre-determined. To account for when and where it will explode we must explain the mechanisms, or causal relations and powers inherent in the system. The failure of the Gunpowder Plot can only be explained if we account for the substances in the system; the chemical (gunpowder), the agents (Fawkes and his associates), an anonymous tip-off to the 4th Baron Monteagle, and the structures (King James I and the guards he sent to search the cellars of Parliament, and who subsequently arrested Fawkes).

Every English child knows the story of Guy Fawkes and his failed attempt to blow up the English Parliament. We persist in burning Fawkes' effigy on the 5th of November and sing the nursery rhyme 'Remember, remember, the 5th of November, gunpowder, treason, and plot … '; and for those who are unfamiliar with this story, substitute any recent act of terrorism, most likely planned with more sophisticated explosives. The underlying realist account remains the same. An explosive outcome is not pre-determined, but determined by powers and liabilities. These physical, social, and structural mechanisms all have to be disclosed for the explosion to happen. As with the disclosure of mechanisms to realise the explosive potential of gunpowder, sampling in qualitative research discloses a range of powers or liabilities as mechanisms for it to happen. Some of these mechanisms are external powers to the research and others internal. In identifying these we are able to elaborate on how these powers inform and control choices about who or what we want and are able to sample in the research.

It is tempting to draw on a metaphor of Russian dolls to explain this disclosure, in which the various physical, social, and structural mechanisms nest within the others to realise a particular sample in research. But the traditional *matryoshka* doll, where each is a scaled up version of its smaller sibling does not quite work as an adequate metaphor. More modern *matryoshka* dolls, such as those readily available in the markets behind Red Square, which nest a doll of Lenin, within a representation of Stalin, and so on all the way to Vladimir Putin, better explain the internal and external powers and liabilities

75

that must be disclosed to interpret and explain social process and social objects in realist research. Vladimir Vladimirovich Putin is Vladimir Ilyich Lenin's heir, even though many of the powers and dispositions that connect them are certainly not visible. Similarly, researchers are asked to explain the powers, dispositions, and liabilities that frame the choice of cases in research. Researchers can never be fully reflexive of course, an issue discussed in the conclusion to this chapter, but their challenge is to disclose the external and internal powers of sampling in the research as best they can.

External and internal powers in sampling

External powers are contingent to sampling. They are tangential, touching upon the sampling and the research, exerting their liabilities in particular ways, and shaping or defining the possibilities for a sample to be chosen or controlled by researchers. The institutions for whom we do research – universities, funding bodies, research governance structures, ethical review bodies, and so on – have powers to define the kinds of research that are possible, the research topics we may investigate, and the ways in which these are investigated. These mechanisms govern the kinds of research that can be done, and therefore the research questions we may ask. Subsequently, the samples we may choose to answer these research questions are described through powers and liabilities. Our sample is an outcome contingent upon external relations, which are embodied in the institutions for whom we do research.

In a similar way, a gatekeeper in the research has the determined potential power to shape who we may or may not talk with, thus shaping the possibilities for research. This determined power, is, like the explosive potential of gunpowder, not pre-determined. We may spend considerable resources developing a relationship of trust and negotiating a different outcome to the one the gatekeeper first intended. Nonetheless, gatekeepers have liabilities (and are often seen as a liability to the research), through refusing introductions or ensuring the researchers talk to particular kinds of people or access particular resources, which allow them to control the sample in particular ways.

External liabilities have a significant impact on the choices that can be made about who or what to sample in the research. These powers and liabilities can modify each other as well. That a researcher is seen as representing a particular institution could, potentially, fashion the ways in which gatekeepers respond to researchers seeking access to a sample through their mediation, for instance. That I work for a large university in a northern English city can be seen to confer credibility and legitimacy with some audiences. With others, the institution for which I work may well be perceived as a distant, irrelevant, ivory tower that does not address their needs.

Powers are relational, they are also wide ranging. Wendy Olsen (2004) describes how her association with low-caste women in a village in Andhra Pradesh, India, barred her from talking with higher caste women and their husbands, for instance. These external powers are mechanisms that allow for one sample in the research at the possible expense of a quite different one. These external powers motivate, constrain, discourage, and enable certain sorts of samples, they interpose in the choices to sample in particular ways.

The powers and liabilities of the caste system in rural India are built on ideas of touchability, untouchability, and the possibilities of transmission through a third person, for instance. In describing our sampling choices we will be interested to record these contingent experiences and events and how these frame in some way the possibilities to form a sample. There is invariably an element of constrained choice in the sampling choices we can make.

Unlike external powers, the generative mechanisms internal to the study are not contingent. These are the sets of ideas, or theories made by researchers that inform the choice of sample. Internal powers are explicitly theory laden. They have the potential to modify the sample chosen in quite significant and fundamental ways.

This theoretical reflexivity is, of course, evident in many reports from qualitative research. An example that exemplifies this approach is an investigation of consumption patterns, lifestyles, and local belonging within the middle class conducted by Mike Savage, Gaynor Bagnall, and Brian Longhurst (2005). Early in their account of this research these authors note that there is a renewed recognition among social scientists of the salience of class identity. This is part of a minor revival of interest in class within the discipline of Sociology, where class identities had for some time been downplayed at the expense of the investigation of other dimensions of identity such as gender, ethnicity, sexuality and locale. This study is positioned within a theoretical literature, in particular an employment aggregate approach to class analysis, and the effect class position within employment has on life-chances, educational achievement, and political orientation. Furthermore, alongside Savage's scholarship on class identities, the study is framed in the theoretical positions of the other two researchers' concerns with consumption in local contexts. Drawing on these theoretical positions and insights from Pierre Bourdieu, into how people feel comfortable or not in any particular local contexts, these researchers made choices about the places around the city of Manchester in the UK in which they would focus their sampling.

Exemplified in this account are the generative mechanisms that govern the sample. A structural and external power is described in framing the study within a wider account about the salience of class identity within the discipline of Sociology. This is a contingent generative mechanism, which is a relatively enduring and identifiable tendency at play in framing the study in a particular way. Done in another time, place, or discipline then it is likely that other choices may well have been made for the focus of the study. This account also shows the ways in which Mike Savage and his colleagues bring their theoretical and conceptual presuppositions to bear in framing the study and, therefore, the sample.

The linguistic fallacy in describing samples

When a sample is described in a monograph, published or working paper, thesis, or dissertation it most often describes the people or things included in the study. This description relates an account of something that is tangible and empirical. Here, for instance, is a description from the methods used in research investigating networks, neighbourhoods, and communities, which is typical of the way in which a sample is often presented:

> We identified four groups (within a geographic area). students; long-term residents living in less affluent circumstances; ethnic minority groups (in particular Pakistani groups whose family origin was in North-West Pakistan, and Afro-Caribbean groups); and young professionals. As with any research project, we were constrained in the resources available. Decisions were made early in the research about how many individuals we could sample. Resources allowed for the inclusion of 24 participants, we selected six from each of the four groups, though it is important to recognise that our sampled groups are not necessarily mutually exclusive (Emmel and Clark, 2009: 5–6).

Descriptions of samples that provide only this empirical insight display a linguistic fallacy in that they mistake this language about the samples' being for adequate explanation of its being. What is missing from this account, and I hasten to add can be found elsewhere (Clark, 2007), are the theoretical assumptions that were marshalled to arrive at decisions about how the sample was chosen in a particular geographical space, why sampling these groups was considered a legitimate way to gain insight into networks, neighbourhoods, and communities, and the ways in which these three contested terms were understood theoretically in the research. In other words, how the research was framed by assumptions, which had their expression as sets of ideas or theories in the research. These were the internal powers of generative mechanisms, which in turn led to sampling choices in this research.

Generative mechanisms, as discussed at the beginning of the chapter, refer to something that is real. They are both contingent and external, and theoretical and internal. When recognised in this way, they allow researchers to explain the causal processes that govern the salient features of the sample, or its regularity in the research. It is to the practical implications of this conceptualisation of sampling that this discussion now turns. The focus is on how samples are used in research towards generating knowledge. In a realist sampling strategy purposive work leads to purposeful sampling choices.

Purposive work and purposeful choices

A scientific realist sampling strategy is driven through sets of ideas (or theories) about the social world we seek to investigate in a particular context. This theoretical understanding is invariably expressed in the early part of the research as research questions, which describe particular theoretical assumptions to be tested and refined. These frame the choices made about who or what to sample in the research.

We commonly think of the units to be sampled through the common idiom of qualitative research, naturalistic enquiry. This resonates at some level in all qualitative research. The focus is on particular cases, be these individual biographies, collective accounts, animate or inanimate evidence that provides rich insight into events and experiences. These cases are bounded in particular ways that allow us to understand how and why they happen in specifiable contexts. Robert Ezra Park, one of the founders of the Chicago School (of Sociology), encouraged his students to go looking for these events and experiences. Get away from your desks he implored:

> You have been told to go grubbing in the library, thereby accumulating a mass of notes and a liberal coating of grime. You have been told to choose problems wherever you can find musty stacks of routine records based on trivial schedules prepared by tired bureaucrats and filled out by reluctant applicants for aid or fussy do-gooders or indifferent clerks. This is called "getting your hands dirty in real research." Those who thus counsel you are wise and honourable; the reasons they offer are of great value. But one thing is more needful; first-hand observation. Go and sit in the lounges of the luxury hotels and on the doorsteps of the flophouses; sit on the Gold Coast settees and on the slum shakedowns; sit in the Orchestra Hall and in the Star and Garter Burlesk (sic). In short, gentlemen, go get the seats of your pants dirty in real research. (Robert E. Park quoted in Hammersley, 1989: 76)

We might question Park's juxtaposition of the (then) smoky burlesque and the library. Sampling choices may include either or both, but the point that naturalistic primary observation is central to learning about events and experiences in particular contexts is an important one. This pragmatic naïve realism must be treated with caution, however, because what is not evidenced in

Park's injunction is to first consider on what theoretical basis choices are made to get one's pants dirty.

This lack of theoretical guidance is expressed in more recent accounts, in particular the strategies of convenience sampling in grounded theory approaches discussed in the case of grounded theory (Chapter 1). Convenience sampling, according to Morse (2007) selects participants because they are accessible. This sampling is used at the beginning of the research to identify the 'scope, major components, and trajectory of the overall process' (2007: 235), in other words, to provide an overview. Researchers are advised to proceed with purposeful sampling once this overview is achieved. This advice, like Robert Park's, is to find people where they are having the experiences you are broadly interested to learn about. As Morse (2007) goes on to suggest, if you are interested in how people use sports facilities in some particular way, go to sports halls; in people's socialising and drinking habits, go to pubs; in how pupils interact with teachers, go to classrooms; in how people with a particular health problem access health services, go to a support group for people with this health problem; and if such places do not exist, then seek out participants through advertising.

Morse's account of convenience sampling is very different to the convenience sampling Patton and Mason caution against researchers using (see Chapters 2 and 3), it is directed rather than *ad hoc*. The advice is neat and has a compelling logic to it. For realists, however, it has an important limitation. It assumes that theories will emerge from close examination of broadly-defined phenomena in their natural setting, with a hope that focus will follow through the recording of incidents, their categorisation, and hypothesis testing to direct theoretical sampling.

Researchers doing purposive work in a realist sampling strategy will spend a considerable amount of time thinking about where the phenomenon they are interested in investigating is most likely to occur. But, unlike in an objectivist grounded theory approach, their approach is not one of convenience. It is the purposeful choice of sampling units, underwritten with presuppositions and ideas as bold conjectures. They are the internal powers that inform choices.

This purposive work does not preclude opportunistic or pragmatic sampling. Researchers are often faced with opportunities in their fieldwork to choose a person, organisation, or object to be sampled. These choices are made with direct reference to the purposive work; a choice is made because it is thought that the inclusion of this unit in the research will allow for the refining and elaboration of theory. Opportunistic sampling emphasises the ways in which purposive work is the act of working out the relation between ideas and evidence and the creative ways in which researchers shape choices about whom or what to sample throughout the research.

In recognising the extent of the purposive work that precedes sampling, be this carefully planned or an opportunistic response to circumstances during fieldwork, a realist sampling strategy may stand charged on merely verifying or forcing the researchers' sets of ideas. As noted from the work of Glaser and Strauss (1967) in case one, verification is seen by many qualitative researchers as both anathema and nemesis. Verification is a very weak argument indeed and, as shown in Chapter 1, has its roots in positivism. The notion that in bringing ideas to research, researchers are merely verifying preconceptions, is further undermined if the purpose of qualitative research is explanation and interpretation. Choosing cases is strongly implicated in these strategies, which require adjudication between theories brought to the investigation. It is to these acts of interpretation and explanation that the discussion now turns.

Strong interpretation and explanation

For Sayer (2000: 17), 'meaning has to be understood, it cannot be measured or counted'. We cannot simply 'read-off' from our various methods the truth about the meanings of the social world. The researcher, as analyst, adjudicates between different sets of ideas. These judgements are interpretations and will always have a hermeneutic element, of which, as Berth Danermark and colleagues (1997) consider, there are two parts. First, this analysis brings the researchers' prejudices and prejudgements, theories, frames of reference, and concepts into engagement with the evidence collected in the research. The second part of this hermeneutic analysis is the interplay between the parts and the whole. Causal explanations of social phenomena require an engagement between the events and experiences recorded and the contexts within which they happen. As Bob Carter and Caroline New (2004: 3) observe, 'we can hope to understand people's options in relation to (the material setting and the cultural meanings of social practice) and their reasons for acting in the ways they do'. Realist research seeks explanations of the concrete, the synthesis of the diverse, which represents a unity of diverse aspects. This interpretation is not reducible, nor is it equivalent, to a descriptive empirical account.

The implications of these observations for sampling are twofold. First, and as discussed above, researchers will always bring prejudices and prejudgements, theories, frames of reference, and concepts to the choices made as to who or what to sample. Secondly, if we are to interpret from the accounts of events and experiences gained from our sample, then we need more than just accounts from the units (or objects) we have chosen to sample. We need, in some way, to be able to understand the contexts within which these objects are described. For Sayer (1992: 116), this strong interpretation (or abstraction):

> analyses objects in terms of their constitutive structures, as parts of wider structures and in terms of their causal powers. Concrete research looks at what happens when these combine.

The context of social life is an open system. A favoured example used by realists is that of the banking system. If one were to try to explain banking to a person from a distant and isolated island you would eventually end up trying to explain the whole of the capitalist system. Clearly, this openness of causal powers is impractical in the kinds of explanation, interpretation, and knowledge generation we undertake in a piece of qualitative research. While we conduct research in an open system in which the generative mechanisms we study interact with other mechanisms, we are obliged to simplify the empirical realities we study. Or as Danermark and colleagues (1997: 199) explain, research must 'reduce in thought the complex empirical reality'. The scope of investigation is limited in some way, producing an ecologically bounded case with its social and institutional norms, values, and inter-relationships (Pawson and Tilley, 1997; Harvey, 2009). An ecologically bounded case produces an identity. It is an expression of connections and context.

At the same time, we are reminded that the ecologically bounded case is part of a much larger whole. It has ontological interconnectedness. We may go as far as to observe that all living and non-living things are an integral part of a social web. Investigations are conducted in an open system. As emphasised, choices are made to limit context and the generative mechanisms investigated if anything useful is to be said about the social world under investigation.

Nonetheless, a realist investigation rejects an atomistic and individualistic account of sampled units, preferring and encouraging explanations and interpretation of the relationships between the parts and the whole. But, as argued, the aim is not holistic descriptions.. The extent of that which is being investigated will always be constrained. Sampling is always a compromise; we must limit the extent of investigation to make it practical and possible. But the descriptions with their limitations, 'provide', as Emma Uprichard (2013a: 375) observes, 'the soil from which causal models of inquiry can germinate and grow'. In being aware of the limits imposed through sampling we are guided as to the claims that can be made from the research. Strong interpretation and explanation seek to disclose the causal powers that are the social phenomenon under investigation. These acts of interpretation and explanation are limited by the boundaries imposed on them in the research. Our claims from the research and the claims to knowledge we are able to produce are similarly limited and bracketed.

Choosing cases – pre-specification and emergence

Realism thrives on counter-instances, events and experiences that are anomalies to be explained and integrated into a theory about a phenomenon. Sampling is the strategy in the research that is used towards building a system through which sets of ideas can be judged, verified, refined, or indeed, ejected wholesale. The key emphasis here is not on controlling the accounts of phenomena through identifying the special typical case and inferring from this case to general theory applied to an emergent universe in the research (see Chapter 3). In a realist strategy, purposeful choices explicitly and strategically bring cases into engagement with one another and with wider social processes in which they occur towards the act of producing theory.

The search is always on to identify cases that are information rich and, if it is possible, can be strategically compared in some way or another. Here we are reminded of Patton's 14+1 strategies for purposeful sampling (discussed in Chapter 2).

A realist strategy differs from Patton's pragmatic account of purposeful sampling, however. Judgements to use these creative strategies in the research are for theoretical rather than empirical reasons. Patton (2002) describes how he might purposefully select a small number of poor families to understand the effectiveness of a programme to reach lower socio-economic groups, for instance. A realist sampling strategy would approach this selection rather differently. Ideas about how the programme was intended to reach these families would be generated first, which in turn will direct sampling. The realist sample is always bootstrapped with theory.

Constructing samples

Ideas drive forward sampling choices. These 'refer to (not "reflect" or "correspond to") real phenomena, rather than abstractions from sense data or to our own constructions' (Maxwell, 2012: 22 – emphasis in the original). Choosing cases in realist qualitative research relies on these weak constructions, these referents to real phenomena, to proceed.

Carolyn Oliver (2012) has argued that later constructivist accounts of grounded theory offer a closer connection to realist sampling strategies. She points out that constructivist grounded theorists (discussed in Chapter 1) may use theoretical constructions as points of departure, which are not the concerns of the participants in the research. According to Charmaz (2006: 10), the theoretical renderings offered by a constructivist grounded theory approach are constructed from 'past and present involvement with people, perspectives, and research practices'. Arising out of these engagements this approach to grounded theory produces abstractions that are claimed to reflect and correspond to empirical reality.

This overarching constructivism from sense data leads to a weakness of approach. As Charmaz (2006) herself notes, many grounded theory studies are descriptive. Her solution to this problem lies in extending the descriptive power of analysis through theoretical sampling in axial coding, with a focus on actions (or process as was noted in Chapter 1) rather than themes. For realists the solution does not lie in returning to the empirical data in the hope of finding new emergent theory, but in the interpretative work that links ideas and evidence to explain real phenomena.

As an example, a well elaborated example of constructivist theoretical sampling is provided by Judith Wuest and colleagues (2002), who investigated the interplay of women's health and social policy within women's lives. The two-stage study investigated how single mothers who left abusive relationships addressed their family's health promotion. From this study they describe an emergent theory, which they call intrusion. This theoretical abstraction includes continuing harassment from the partner, the health consequences of the abuse, costs associated with seeking help, and undesirable changes in living after leaving the abusive partner. In a second stage the researchers identified 'structural domains' (2002: 803) that were implicated in some way in families' experiences of intrusion. To extend the scope of this category, they theoretically sampled service providers and policy makers. They describe this theoretical sampling thus:

> In order to guide theoretical sampling, data analysis occurred concurrently with data collection and had four main thrusts. First, ... describe the services and policy systems in each (Canadian) province. Next we identified the key properties of the services and policy systems that influenced how families promote their health. ... By drawing on these properties, it was possible to identify system strengths and limitations at a thematic level. The final step will be theoretical integration of the properties of each domain into the basic social process (of intrusion) through constant comparison (Wuest et al., 2002: 805).

This is a classic account of theoretical sampling in grounded theory. There is a progression from descriptive themes to the properties of categories for integration and elaboration of the emergent theory, through constant comparison. What is also noticeable is how close the theoretical sampling stays to empirical sense data. The aim of this theoretical sampling in axial coding is to elaborate and enrich the construction of the emergent theory of intrusion.

But, towards the end of the paper, this construction starts to fall apart, revealing the weakness of theoretical sampling that is exclusively reliant on strong constructions from the analysis of sense data. The authors note that abused women who are applying for housing are not asked about the abuse they have suffered, despite the housing service giving priority to abused women who have left their partners; and go on to observe that '[t]here is also an unwritten assumption [in public housing services] that women who are abused will apply for housing from the shelter system, and this is always a necessary condition, but no guarantee, for getting priority (in housing provision)' (2002: 806). They have uncovered a generative mechanism, a real power with causal efficacy, not a constructed theory as to how housing policy is realised.

Earlier in their paper, Wuest and colleagues (2002: 801) contend that they have:

> developed a theory [about social determinants of health and women's health] that was useful to women for understanding their experience and helpful to providers by indicating points of intervention, but that lacked detail needed to really be useful for influencing health and social policy.

Their progress in the study is from this theory of the middle range to quite specific generative mechanisms.

Throughout the paper these authors wonder if they are complying with the rules of grounded theory approaches. They conclude that they have had to take risks with their method and may well have strayed from Glaser and Strauss's approach.

These concerns might have been waylaid if the difference between theoretical sampling in both a positivist and constructivist grounded theory approach and realist account of sampling had been acknowledged, with theory regarded as being in relation to evidence, rather than as an emergent property of the data.

In a realist account of the research, theory, like the generative mechanism of the way in which housing is allocated to abused women who have left their partners, is ontologically real. Explanation and interpretation in a realist sampling strategy tests and refines theory. Sampling choices seek out examples of mechanisms in action, or inaction towards being able to say something explanatory about their causal powers. Sampling, as Matthew Miles and Michael Huberman (1994) suggest, is both pre-specified and emergent, it is driven forward through an engagement with what is already known about that which is being investigated and ideas catalysed through engagement with empirical accounts.

Reflexivity in a realist sampling strategy

In making choices, researchers have a standpoint towards the sample we choose in the research. The powers and liabilities of sampling are from three sources.

First, the sets of ideas, presuppositions, or theories brought to the research by researchers that frame the sample. Secondly, the institutions and the social contexts acting as external powers within which we do research, which, as Tim May with Beth Perry (2011: 5) assert, have the potential to influence 'the process, product, and interpretation of research itself'. Research will always be shaped and critically reviewed by the scientific communities within which we do this research. And thirdly, the ongoing working through of insights from evidence and researchers' conjectures, presuppositions, and propositions that make up the acts of explanation and interpretation. There is a feedback loop between these ideas and events and experiences obtained in the research. The sample is reshaped and reconceptualised in light of these accounts.

These powers and liabilities are at play in framing, shaping, and refining the sample throughout the research. Researchers are always in some position or other in relation to our sample in the research, as Sayer (2000) observes. We therefore require reflexivity that can attempt to grasp the salient features of our sample towards providing a practically adequate account. One challenge we face in a reflexive practice of realist sampling is, of course, that we can never know all of the theory we bring to research. Nor will we ever be able to adequately explain all the presuppositions that we make in our sampling choices. An understanding of context, including the political and socio-cultural contexts of academic life, can only ever be a partial account; however detailed we might make this description. For Mason (2007), to claim more is anti-historical, placing a huge burden on the idea that a researcher can be successfully and extensively reflexive.

This is to recognise the partiality and fallibility of researchers' accounts of the chosen cases – and furthermore, the critical scientific environment within which they are produced. Throughout this chapter the emphasis has been on the weak construction of sampling, the fallibility of knowledge, and ongoing interpretation and explanation of real phenomena. Moreover, it is through recognising that reflexivity is explicit in the research process that it is possible to understand sampling as a product of particular accounts brought to the research. These go some way to disclosing the researchers' power and responsibilities in the research, the institutional contexts in which the research and its sample are generated, and the extent to which our sampling can elaborate the social process we are interested to learn about.

These reflexive engagements are mobilised to avoid, as Gillian Rose (1997: 306) observes, 'the false neutrality and universality of so much of academic knowledge'. Sampling strategies should position knowledge, allowing certain claims to be made that are theoretical. Sampling choices, the theories that informed these, the ways in which these choices are mobilised to test and refine theory, and the boundaries of context cast long shadows across the possible claims from research.

However powerful we may think our analytic powers to be, creating a comprehensive account of our reflexive practice in research, how we have talked to, confronted or acquiesced to power, what we understand to be context, and how participants and researchers have engaged in the research, as examples, is a massive undertaking. To assert that researchers can capture this reflexivity, to make it transparent in the research, is presumptuous. We should simply not imagine that we can know fully both ourselves as social researchers and social actors in the research and beyond, and the context of our research.

These considerations of reflexivity reinforce the observation that sampling is not procedural. These processes cannot be predicted in advance, nor do they conform to rules. They are matters of judgement made by researchers. The uncertainties and complexities of doing research are emphasised. We may accept, reject, or most likely refine theory through the theoretical work of sampling that happens in the research. This sifting, winnowing, and subsequent refining of theory advocated in a scientific realist sampling strategy cannot be described by rules of engagement with data and evidential account. Reflexive practice in sampling can only be shaped by guidelines of practice towards the task of knowledge production.

Our sample is not, as in an analytic inductive strategy, seeking to represent a population in some way. It is concerned to disclose mechanisms, as refined theories that explain social processes. This work will be located in particular, institutional, spatial, temporal, and social boundaries that will be theoretically defined. Explanations will, to return to the intended theoretical account suggested by Glaser and Strauss (1967), be theories of the middle range. As Raymond Boudon (1991) suggests, these theories are what other sciences simply call 'theory'. They are a set of statements that 'organise a set of hypotheses and relate them to segregated observations' (1991: 520). Our theories are valid, yet provisional, if they explain and federate otherwise segregated empirical regularities of that which is investigated and the ways in which the investigation has been conducted. The next chapter uses these observations to understand their implications in doing sampling in qualitative research. The focus is purposive work in realist sampling; work we may describe as getting out of the swamp.

5

PURPOSIVE WORK IN A REALIST SAMPLING STRATEGY

This chapter considers the purposive work of realist sampling strategies, how this work is directed and re-cast through the presuppositions we bring to the research, alongside the external powers and liabilities we reflexively account for in research. Considerable intellectual work is done in the very early stages of our research, when plans are no more than ideas jotted down on the first page of a new notebook. Based on our theoretical understanding of the world, gained through our education, life-experiences, our interaction with the social world, the scholarly communities and research networks of which we are part we think that it is worthwhile doing a particular piece of research. Internal generative mechanisms will be brought to bear on the choices we make about whom or what to sample. Additionally, we will also seek, as best we can, to disclose the contingent powers and liabilities that shape the research, and by extension our sampling choices. These early processes of intellectual and reflexive engagement with the research problem are often described as scoping exercises. A far better metaphor for these processes, I contend, is getting out of the swamp. The work of getting out of the swamp is an effort every qualitative researcher undertakes. Few, it must be said, make much of this process in reports from research, perhaps feeling that giving an account of this work goes against the grain of grounded theory approaches to research. But when it is honestly reported it makes eminent sense.

Getting out of the swamp

We spend a great deal of time at the beginning of any piece of research getting out of the swamp. As Trisha Greenhalgh (2008) observes, this work is uniquely unpredictable, uniquely frustrating, and uniquely time consuming. We do not know the width or depth of the research problem we are setting out to research.

Consider if you will, the first meeting with an undergraduate student who is planning her final year degree dissertation. She arrives for the meeting with an idea – 'I want to research … '. This is an idea that she forms, based on a topic that has fired her imagination during her course, experiences in her own life, or even something she has read about in a newspaper that strikes her as an important social issue to understand better. Her ideas about what to research are mediated through the discipline of which she is part. For Andrew Abbott (2001: 130) '[d]isciplines provide dreams and models of reality and learning. They create modes of knowledge that seem to the participants, uniquely real.' Of necessity and through the scope of their teaching and learning the many disciplines that make up the modern university legitimise partial knowledge. But, academic disciplines are not the product of myopic reflection within the ivory tower. Research, and the disciplines within which it is conceived and executed, are 'implicated in new forms of governmentality, regulation, and social imaginary' (Savage, 2010: 68). The partiality of discipli-nary knowledge and its interaction with real-world problems is expressed in the internal and external powers and liabilities, or generative mechanisms. These shape the possibilities for research. They organise a system of meanings within social and institutional norms, values, and inter-relationships, which govern the kinds of research topics we choose.

Generative mechanisms are more than just an expression of disciplinary boundaries and borderlands, however. Supervision will encourage our student to think about resources first. We will remind her that she is limited by time and word-count. Superficially we are encouraging her to think about how she is constrained in particular ways as to what she can tackle in her research project. We are also pointing to the generative mechanisms that shape the proposed research. In addition, even at this early stage of our supervision we will, undoubtedly, encourage our student to think carefully who the audience is for her research. We are asking her to reflect on the contingent relationships within which the research can be conducted and the kinds of claims she will be able to make from the research.

These questions are not only practical ones, but remind us that all research is framed in particular ways by the institutions for whom we do research, which may be embodied in tutors and examiners in the university, by fund-ing agencies, governments, or clients who commission research from us. All of these shape the possibilities for research through defining a particular context, the questions we may ask of the social world, the kinds of research that can be done, the audiences we propose to share our research with, and what they will consider credible research. These considerations impact on the design of the research. There is a strong relationship between resource issues, ethical considerations, and institutional demands for any piece of research. Our view of these impact on the choice of sample, with whom or what, and when we may use sampling strategies.

Before our student can decide (and have decided for her) who or what she will sample, she must be able to explain to herself the reasons for selecting a particular sample. She must arrive at bold theoretical conjectures to inform her purposive sampling strategy. Towards this end, as supervisors we may advise her to focus her ideas in a particular direction. But, in a pedagogic environment where academic freedom wins out over prescriptions, these will be gentle nudges. The strong messages we will convey are always the same; be creative and careful, search the bibliographic databases, go to the library, and look beyond its dusty shelves into the world in which the social process is happening. Listen to the ways in which politicians talk about it on the morning news, read about how journalists report it in newspapers, read the microblogs, and talk with people who know about it. In short, search for the ways in which events and experience are expressed, and how these are explained. Bundled into these explanations are the generative mechanisms, the real ideas about how a process works, in what circumstances, for whom, when, and why. We will ask our student to consider who or what will provide an opportunity to test and refine theory most effectively.

Even at this very early stage in the research, when our ideas are no more than a few scribbles in what will soon become a research diary, the design of the research is being informed by theories. We neither encourage our students to enter the field, nor do we approach research with only a general sociological understanding of the research problem. This does not mean that we are entering into research with immutable theories to be verified, nor does it imply that we are theoretically insensitive. In fact, quite the opposite is happening. A reflexive engagement with the research problem means we are engaging with accounts of events and experiences, and identifying generative mechanisms through interpretation that we propose will bring about particular regularities and outcomes in specified contexts. These are theoretical constructs, but of the weakest kind, because they will have real consequences and outcomes. They provide the framework for the interpretation that will happen in the research. Additionally, they are the ideas that will inform early sampling strategies in the research. These ideas will be subject to review throughout the research. The sample we choose based on this uniquely challenging work is the bearer of ideas we investigate in the research.

One source of inspiration for us and our students will inevitably be research done by other researchers. These investigations provide insight into the ways in which particular problems have been conceptualised: the ideas that framed their study; the contingent powers that shaped the study in a particular time and place; and, through these considerations, the sample chosen in the research as the bearer of the claims from that research. In order to get out of the swamp and climb to the higher ground from which to get a better view of how we will conduct research and choose cases, we will need to ask about conceptual framework, theoretical presuppositions, and external powers that shaped the research we review; getting out of the swamp demands processes of interpretation and theory building that rely on the description, interpretation, and explanation from past research.

Why the Lynds chose the sample they did in the Middletown studies: interpretation and theory building

Getting out of the swamp, as the previous section shows, requires theoretical insights, interpretation, and reflexivity. As an example of how this may happen, Robert S. Lynd and Helen Merrell Lynd's studies of Middletown (1929, 1937) provide useful insight into the nature of the internal and external powers in shaping a sample. Its value as a case study is strengthened because others have come after the Lynds and directly confronted the assumptions that informed the choice of sample in the original studies.

Middletown, (Muncie, Indiana) was selected by the Lynds and their co-researchers because they claimed it shared many features of a wide group of American cities of its time. The period of the study (1890 and 1924) were captured in the dynamic development of this mid-American city, in which:

> This narrow strip of thirty-five years comprehends for hundreds of American communities the industrial revolution that has descended upon villages and towns, metamorphosing them into a thing of Rotary Clubs, central trade councils, and Chamber of Commerce contests for "bigger and better" cities. (1929: 6)

What the Lynds were seeking to capture in their sample was the development of the typical American city at the turn of the nineteenth and at the dawn of the twentieth centuries. To do so required the researchers to theorise what they considered to be a typical American city of the time. The Lynds and their co-researchers chose to sample particular units in the city and, at the same time, ignore other groups that lived there. In the notes on method that accompany the Lynd's first study of Middletown, they note that Middletown is racially homogeneous. A small 'Negro and foreign born population' (1929: 8) is grudgingly accepted to live in the town, but these potential parts of their sample are pushed to one side with an observation that the research was about culture, not race. Investigation of race is left for others to do. Yolanda T. Moses would argue much later that 'the original Middletown study was a metaphor for the invisibility of people of color in the social science literature during the twentieth century' (2004: ix). And, while the proportion of blacks living in Muncie was indeed small in 1924–25, their community was growing at a faster rate, and was larger as a proportion of the population than the cities of Chicago, New York, and Detroit according to Luke Eric Lassiter (2004). The Lynds appeared to wish to ignore the other side of Middletown because the study's focus was on institutions (the ways and mores of working class and business class American families earning their livings, making their homes, bringing up their children, doing leisure, and engaging in religious and community life) which, in the early 1920s, were not considered the habits, habitats, or habitus of African Americans.

What is to be considered typical in the Lynds' study of Middletown is defined and filtered by the ways in which they seek to theoretically frame the study. As interestingly, this observation can be read the other way around. What is theoretically adequate is typical. The typical 1920s American city existed without Black American and foreign-born populations. Or so it was widely held amongst the commentators and social observers of the day. As H. L. Mencken observed in a review of Middletown in the *American Mercury* in 1929 (cited in Igo, 2007: 84), the Lynds 'did not seek the (city) that was most completely typical, but simply the one that was as thoroughly American as possible'. This Americanism was an idea. It excluded the black and foreign born population. The fieldwork was done in Muncie in the same year as the Johnson–Reed Act was implemented, which excluded immigrants from Asian, East Asian, Southern and Eastern Europe. Sarah Igo (2007) notes the uneasiness amongst what she describes as *genus Americanus* – white and Western European in origin – in a time of the ascendancy of the Ku Klux Klan, scientific eugenics, heightened racial nationalism, and urbanisation. This is not to suggest that the Lynds set out with racist views in the design of their research – they may or may not have, and it is not possible to understand this from what they present. They simply ignored the black and foreign communities of Muncie. What this study reveals are the ways in which the sample is a sample in its time, a sample that reflects powers and liabilities expressed in a particular moment. As Igo (2007: 85) observes of the study of Middletown:

> native white subjects could embody America, while black and immigrant Americans could only represent themselves. A general public fascination with social science thus coexisted seamlessly with a decidedly unscientific notion of representativeness.

If we roll the clock forward to 2004, *The other side of Middletown: Exploring Muncie's African American Community* is researched in a rather different historical epoch, as Hurley Goodall and Elizabeth Campbell (2004) show. The African American communities of Muncie can no longer be ignored. Other powers shape the possibilities for research; the Civil Rights Movement and the demand of African Americans to be heard prevail. The omission of Muncie's black community from the Lynds' study would be addressed, first through the activism of a former union leader, Hurley Goodall, who collaborated with a

Ball State University professor to write a history of Muncie's African American population (Lassiter, 2012). Growing out of this collaboration, activists, faculty, and students went on to investigate the other side of Middletown using innovative methods and sampling strategies.

Powers and liabilities contingent to the research shape the possibilities of the sample. In 1979, two Ball State University professors, C. Warren Vander Hill and Dwight W. Hoover conducted nineteen interviews with Jewish residents of Muncie (Rottenberg, 1997). In *Middletown in Transition* (Lynd and Merrell Lynd, 1937) the Lynds note a small population of Jews and a synagogue in Muncie, but they were 'a very inconspicuous factor of Middletown' (1937: 313). Dwight W. Hoover (in the introduction to Rottenberg, 1997) considers the Lynds' failure to study the Jews in Middletown unsurprising. He identifies three reasons. First, the funders of the Middletown study, the Institute of Social and Religious Research, requested a survey of an entire community's religious practices with an overarching goal of uniting all Protestant churches in the country, which straight away excluded certain groups from the sample. Secondly, as already noted, the study was framed by a notion of what constituted *genus Americanus* circa 1920 – homogeneous, white, and Western European. And thirdly, Hoover points to Robert Lynd's theoretical orientation, in which religion was sidelined in preference for processes of modernity. American society was best modelled through an understanding of large manufacturing. Those owning and working in this manufacturing were the key focus of investigation at the expense of small retail businesses, where many of the Jews were employed. The sample in the Lynds' study is not a pristine unadulterated product of empirical observation. It is continually informed, as all studies are, by the contingent powers and liabilities that shape the sample. The sample reflects funders', researchers', and the wider societies' image of American society in the late 1920s.

Lynd and Merrell Lynd (1929: 507) assume a homogeneous *genus Americanus*, which is invoked in the identification of the sample:

> The requirement in the selection of these families were that they be native-born, white Americans, that they live within the city limits, that both parents be alive and living together, and they have one or more children between the ages of six and eighteen years (1929: 507).

A theory of the homogeneity of that which is to be sampled is reinforced in the procedure of sampling. The working class group, for instance, which the Lynds considered the most representative of their two samples of *genus Americanus*, was drawn from the payrolls in the three major manufacturing plants in the town.

As the studies of Middletown from the 1920s to the present day show, the choice of what to sample is continually guided by generative mechanisms. The Lynds' study of Muncie exemplifies the ways in which these external and internal powers and liabilities come into play with the choice of sample. Researchers are constantly guided and constrained by what can be researched in the institutions within which research is funded and conducted. Studies are rooted in their times and places. The samples chosen have properties expressed through these generative mechanisms. These are applied in particular and practical ways in the research and find their expression in the design of research and the choices researchers are directed to make about whom or what to sample through the intention to test and refine theory. Interpretation of past studies supports the processes of producing ideas as real generative mechanisms to be tested and refined in our research. A challenge faced within any research is how to produce a coherent strategy, that links generative mechanisms to method and procedure and through which to say something useful about the questions being asked of the social world. In part, I suggest, this theorisation arises from the reports from empirical studies of the past. They provide a historical bedrock for theory building. But theories do not merely fall out of past studies, they come from the acts of theorising we carry out as researchers individually and in research teams.

Theories frame sampling choices

Theory always precedes data collection in a scientific realist sampling strategy, or as Michael Buroway (2009: 13) contends 'without theory we are blind – we cannot see the world'. These theories inform the strategies of purposive work because, while constructed, they are nonetheless real in the sense of being and explaining reality. Ideas are, at least provisionally, stable and consequential.

Sampling choices could potentially draw from a wide range of theoretical positions in the research, with different theories having different empirical foci as Buroway goes on to observe. As noted in the discussion of the basics of realist sampling strategies in the previous chapter, throughout the research we will make rational, yet fallible judgements about competing theories, models, and concepts to frame the sample. We will construct sampling strategies through the lens of the theories we bring to the research to be tested and refined. These are constructions which connect theory to sampling choices in the research and as such are weak constructions, but can be well illustrated using the strong constructivism of Gubrium and Holstein (1987), showing how the apparently commonsensical phenomenon of family may be constructed in two quite distinct ways.

Drawing extensively on the evocative language used by Gubrium and Holstein (1987), family may be theorised as the 'final haven of the heart' that is 'sentimental, loyal, protective, and private'. Families can be conceived of as having an 'inside and an outside' in which 'particular ways of regulating and ordering their own inner life and dealing with the outside world' are made. Family life, invoking Elizabeth Bott's pioneering study, which I will return to in Chapter 7, happens 'inside homes' and 'behind closed doors', it is the 'natural and native' setting of the intensely private activity of doing family. A rather different theory of family can position this institution as 'well beyond the limits of households' in which the 'privacies of the household are part and parcel of public issues'. The household is not the 'site of separate and discrete domestic order' but is instead 'a presumed location towards which both members and non-members present, share, and argue social order'. Presented here are two very different constructions of domestic reality, one with a focus on the private, the other seeing the family as part and parcel of public issues. How then might a sample differ in the investigation of family drawing on these two theories? Table 5.1, suggests a sample derived from each of these theoretical positions.

The theories of family suggested in Table 5.1 provide insight into two quite distinct constructions of family. Family, or any object of study for that matter, is conceived through these kinds of descriptive practices. These practices Gubrium and Holstein (1987: 783) contend, emphasising their strongly constructivist position, 'spawns diverse technical and theoretical questions'.

Table 5.1 Sampling the private and public family – the implications of these constructions for sampling strategies

Research questions	The private family	The public family
Location	Those who live within the four walls of a household	The family and individuals and organisations that look in on the family in its geography (e.g. relatives, social workers, doctors)
Familial representation	Family members either individually or collectively, household census data*	The family, those who represent the family to the public sphere (e.g. social workers, probation workers, teachers), legal documents
Assigning meaning	Family members either individually or collectively, artefacts (e.g. family photographs, which may be curated by one or more family members)	The family and professionals with authority to mediate family relationships (e.g. police, judges), judgements as documents

*such data are not available at this level of aggregation but its construction by one or more family members provides a private representation of the family

For realist researchers, however, the constructions we produce in the research are weak. It is not empirical description that leads to theory, but theories that connote the procedures and strategies of sampling. Each or both of the accounts of family, suggested in Table 5.1 may well provide a theoretical account to inform the sampling strategies in the research, an issue I return to in the next chapter in the discussion of purposefully choosing cases. Family may be theorised and understood as private or public, or indeed both, within the context of the research questions being asked. The aim in choosing a sample will be to find units that best allow the testing of theoretical presuppositions.

The best that can be said of these constructions is that they raise consciousness about that which is the focus of study. They are conceptions that refer to real phenomena and social process. They are abstractions neither derived from empirical observation, nor construed from our own constructions. They make theoretical sense in the context of that which we are studying. These ideas may be arrived at through interpretation of everything from a 140 character tweet (microblog) to the (slightly longer and more involved) work of grand-theorists, and anything in between.

We are faced with a further task before we can pull our way out of the swamp. We must bring these ideas into engagement with the corpuscular empirical world we want to investigate. For this we need a way of describing our sample to ourselves and to others. It is the describing of samples that I now consider.

Spatchcocking the variable

The choices about whom or what to sample invariably starts with particular instances (or units). These are most often characterised and described using variables. This is a term cast as anathema to some qualitative researchers (see Chapter 1). But, more often, as noted from the ways in which Patton (2002) uses criteria, including variables, to identify information rich cases, and Mason (2002) suggests their use to make decisions about who or what to strategically sample early in the research, variables are used cautiously and interpretatively, and always with an eye to their imperfections. The reason for this caution, as Mike Savage (2010) observes, is because variables flatten the social world they purport to represent. By assigning a description to something using a variable, there is the potential we may treat all of the instances or units categorised using the variable in the same way, when there may be significant differences between them. Similarly, David Byrne (2002, 2012) contends, variables measure the traces of systems that make up reality.

Despite these limitations, the language of variables and categories is used in both quantitative and qualitative research. They are a common currency of research and, indeed, everyday descriptions of social life. In research, they have one value for each case and vary across the population. This formulation of social phenomena into variables allows for the production of systematic, comprehensive codes that can be described in one coding system. In using variables in this way they take on particular social meanings.

Age can be treated as a variable, for instance. We may ask, 'how old were you at your last birthday?', as might happen in a survey or census. But this question merely reports that which is nominally observable or reported without critically engaging with what the social process of age means, such as the effects of a point in a life cycle, membership of a generation, or the relationship between age and social class.

A variable, like age, will never capture the intimate and inner-moving complex of meanings that underlie social processes. Or, as Herbert Blumer (1956: 685 – emphasis in the original) contends in his classic critique of the variable, its 'relation is a single relation, necessarily stripped bare of the complex things that sustain it in a "here and now" context'. For qualitative researchers, variables can neither adequately express Blumer's notion of the 'here and now context' nor 'the context lying beneath the content' (Pawson, 1989: 72).

Variables are, nonetheless, theory laden, as Cathi Marsh (1982: 59) emphasises:

> all the small decisions about coding and grouping that are made in the course of the (survey) research should *(a)* be recorded and *(b)* be defended according to some theoretical rationale.

The question for realist researchers is how well this theorising of variables cuts reality at its joints. Consider, for instance, the following case. The UK Office for National Statistics (Gooding, 2011) estimates inflation rates using a basket of commonly bought household goods. In 2011, an oven-ready joint of meat replaced 'pork shoulder joint, reflecting a longer-term movement to prepared food' (Table 3 in Gooding 2011). Mobile phone downloads were replaced with mobile phone applications, flat screen televisions were subdivided into three size groups, reflecting the different prices and purchasing choices made by households. As John Lanchester (2012) observes, reading these tables is like reading a novel about domestic habits in twenty-first century Britain. Read across several years of these carefully thought through and chosen variables and one can indeed divine something of the changing habits of the British shopper and the things they buy. But as things they remain discrete, singular lumps, which limit the account of process. They are key concepts, specified through an immediate, intuitive, and empirically derived theory. As Blumer (1956: 684) observes, they are 'constructed to fit the particular problem on which one is working' and are 'localised in terms of their content'. They aid analysis, in this case to produce an index of inflation, but do little to augment interpretation of process beyond this concrete and localised problem.

In a similar way, describing the sample through the language of variables neglects the temporal and contextual accounts of the different powers and liabilities that shape and form this sample. A key concern in describing the sampling choices in research are with a process approach to causality, in which the aim is to open up the black box of assumptions for inspection about whom or what the sample is in the research. For Pawson (1989: 71) this black box is 'quite literally the mental fabrication of path diagrams' that link independent to dependent variables, in which causality is seen as no more than a regularity linking thing to thing. To use David Hume's original description, causality is 'felt by the soul and not perceived externally in bodies ... a secret cause which separates and unites' (Hume, 1949[1817]: 77). Exposing these secrets is the job of experimental induction, and specifically the application of Method of Agreement 'comparing together instances in which the phenomenon does occur' and Method of Difference, 'comparing together instances in which the phenomenon does occur with instances in other respects similar in which it does not' as John Stuart Mill proposed (2005[1886]: 253). These nineteenth century philosophers of method described the canons for experimental design which placed the variable, in its inalienable state, at the epicentre of explanation of the physical and social world.

For many researchers, both quantitative (Byrne, 2002, 2012; Deutsch, 2011) and qualitative, this experimental model will not do. In a realist account of research and sampling, in particular, David Hume's secret cause can be replaced by real causal generative mechanisms. As Pawson and Tilley (1997: 33 – emphasis in the original) assert, 'there is a *real* connection between events which we understand to be causally connected'. For the realist qualitative (and indeed quantitative) researcher the challenge is not to accept the language of variables at face value, nor to assume the causal accounts they carry in their associations as invisible to anything but empirical investigation. Realists recognise that causal powers and liabilities can be described and will be re-described as the powers and liabilities of the sample are better understood in the research.

As discussed in the previous chapter, it will often be the case that an early description of the sample will employ variables. A sample may be described as being made up of eight men with this particular feature, another eight with that particular feature, and so on, for instance. Alongside this description there will already be an account of why the sample was chosen, based on the theoretical work. Moreover, as the research progresses these descriptive variables will be spatchcocked (not the men I hasten to add).

The term spatchcocking, which I borrow from Steven French and James Ladyman (2003), is the act of splitting poultry, generally a chicken, down its breastbone and opening it up to reveal the details of its thoracic and abdominal cavities. In a similar way, in research we will split these things, these variables used to describe our sample, open and lay bare their anatomy for scrutiny and explanation through theorisation and empirical investigation. In the process of which we will be able to better describe, interpret, and, ultimately, explain the sample.

From empirical choices to realist sampling strategies

While recognising the limitations of variables to describe samples, these monadic descriptions inform decisions about whom or what to sample in the early part of research. Units are chosen, but these are only empirical and actual descriptions. These may be people, groups of people, places, organisations, documents, artefacts, webpages, or images, as examples, all of which will have particular characteristics. While, as observed in the previous section, this is a starting point in describing this sample, even at this early stage description and interpretation of the sample chosen goes beyond these variables, to include the underlying mechanisms, the theories as ideas and presuppositions, that have led us to decide which particular units to include in our research.

This approach to the selection of the sample appears similar to the way in which Strauss and Corbin (1990) describe purposeful sampling in open coding (see Chapter 1). They chose CAT scanners because they are big, expensive, and high status. Strauss and Corbin made their choice through an inductive method of difference and agreement. Their aim was to set the scene for the emergence of theory in the research, which was able to explain causal relationships between what they could see (a big expensive machine) and the ways in which patient care happened and medical personnel did their work through their interaction with this scanner.

The justification for making the choice is different in a realist sampling strategy. It is purposive and made because researchers have an idea, a theory to test, a proposed causal generative mechanism, which presupposes that staff will work in some particular way when they are using this large, high prestige equipment. These theories drive the sampling strategy forward.

Representativeness

The relation between ideas and evidence constantly informs the choice of cases in a realist sampling strategy, the aim of which is to test, refine, and judge ideas which, as was discussed in Chapter 4, are always provisional, because social systems are open. In this way, realist sampling strategies differ significantly from those of analytic inductive approaches, which, as Bhaskar (2008) notes, depend upon closed systems of critical cases, for it is only when a system can be closed down that claims can be made to it being representative of some universe within which specific cases fit.

As an example of how this closure is achieved, Giampietro Gobo (2006), describes conducting a study of call centres in Italy. He wished to learn about customer relationship management practices. He estimated that there were 1020 call centres at the time of his study, falling into three organisational groups; private or marketing orientated; public, such as medical despatch centres; and non-profit. Gobo points out that if he followed a statistical approach to sampling, he would select call centres from these three groups. The organisations would be the focus of the sampling. But his interest is not organisations but the relational practices that happen between call centre operators and customers within these organisations. The focus of his enquiry and the phenomena to be sampled are these relationships, not the call centre organisations. Gobo proceeds by placing this understanding at the heart of his sampling strategy. He sets out to understand the kinds of relational practices that happen between call centre operator and customer.

Gobo emphasises how he undertook literature reviews, talked with experts, and carried out ethnographic research through which he identified four different kinds of relational practice; counselling, marketing, interviewing, and advertising. Given the resources available to him, he decided to investigate one practice in detail, counselling. He set about identifying new accounts, which he found to have considerable variability of counselling practices. His work identifies the empirical contours of his study. These were the focus of his sampling strategies. They relate directly to the theoretical aims in the research and its empirical contours. For Gobo (2006) they start to get at that which is representative – a characteristic of the sample – and, at the same time give priority to relationships rather than individuals, which are the focus of qualitative researching. Gobo's analytic induction leads him from intellectual work and specific empirical observation to claims for critical cases in the research and from these claims to considerations of what these represent.

The traces of real systems

Purposive work in a realist sampling strategy does not seek to identify typical cases, but to identify the traces of real systems. Ideas and accounts of events and experiences, most often presented as variables, are brought together in the purposive work that directs sampling. These traces of real systems may exist in sampling frames, as surveys, census reports, or electoral rolls, for instance. Evidence is brought into relation with the researchers' ideas in choosing cases.

In the last chapter I discussed the theoretical reflexivity Savage and colleagues (2005) applied in deciding who to sample in their study of consumption patterns, lifestyles, and local belonging within the middle class. As noted, their theoretical ideas led them to conclude that the city of Manchester in the UK exemplified particular processes of globalisation they wanted to investigate. Their four case studies chosen in the research are contrasting areas of the city. The choice emphasises the ways in which evidence is brought into relation with ideas.

One case, Chorlton, is selected because it is 'a district of urban gentrification' with 'new cafes, wine bars, restaurants, and specialist shops', which is close to the city centre, yet has a distinct identity because of its geography. It has a 'bohemian feel linked to the existence of its distinctive shopping centre'. Its house prices suggest it is home to professional groups, who have replaced the urban working class population that had lived in the area.

The researchers expected the city and its suburbs to be defined by zones within which residents with different combinations of economic and/or social capital live and form distinct local milieu. Their confidence in the ways in which place might be the focus of an investigation of diversity and particularity amongst a well defined group of the middle class is emphasised through their choice of sampling strategy. Once they had chosen the four areas in which to do the research, they used the electoral register as their sampling frame. From this they selected particular streets and knocked on every third door, alternating their requests for interviews between men and women in each household.

Familiarity with the potential research sites and the city of Manchester in general must have played an important part in the researchers' choices. At the time of the research all three researchers were based at universities in Manchester and its environs. As university lecturers they are middle class too, so will have had a good idea about some of the features of their eventual sample. (I return to the implications of choosing people like us in research in Chapter 7). Some parts of this reflexive engagement will be planned and expressed, other parts will be intuitive. Nonetheless, Savage and colleagues (2005), as I have shown here and in the previous chapter, bring description and interpretation through empirical observation, secondary analysis of quantitative data, and theory into engagement to choose their sample and sampling strategy.

A realist purposive sampling strategy in a Mumbai slum

In any research we must make the unfamiliar familiar to us. The emergent properties of the sample, exposed through getting out of the swamp, are one part of the interpretative strategies in the research through which this happens. A realist sampling strategy brings ideas and accounts of events and experiences together in the purposive work that directs sampling.

Take, for instance, a problem I faced in research investigating perceptions of health and the value placed on health providers in the slums of Mumbai, India (Emmel, 1998). My first visits to the slum, which was chosen for me as much as I chose it through my gatekeeper contacts, were confusing. According to the Census of India, here lived over 18,000 people packed into a small area not much larger than a professional football field, hemmed in on two sides by busy main roads, and on the others by blocks of low-rise flats and wasteland. Hut was crammed next to hut along winding and often steep alleyways. When I looked down on the slum from a nearby tall building it all looked much the same to me, well built clay tiled roofs intermixed with poorly constructed tarpaulin roofed huts in an incomprehensible jumble. There was nothing to distinguish one area of the slum from another. Yet, I knew from talking with community activists and community health workers that the slum was built at different times and made up of different groups.

My guide to starting to understand the slum was theory. Theories of development contend that there is a gradual improvement in the lives of the urban poor in low-income countries over time. A theory of epidemiological transition (Bobadilla et al., 1993), in particular, holds that there is a shift from illness and death associated with infectious diseases, like diarrhoea, malaria, and measles, to chronic non-communicable conditions, like diabetes, heart disease, and stroke. This transition can be accounted for through improvements to the built environment, such as better housing, better service provision including water supply and sanitation, and increasing household wealth and access to health services associated with forces of macro-development. This theory of epidemiological transition informed my first forays into sampling. Equipped with a theory that one should see improved development within the slum over time, should one choose the right indicators, I consulted experts, eight community health workers who live and work in the slum. I was mindful of Blumer's observation that:

> with ingenuity one can impart a quantitative dimension to almost any qualitative item. One can usually construct some kind of measure or index of it to develop a rating scheme for judges. (Blumer, 1956: 683)

Together the community health workers and I produced three scales. The first measured the wealth of the neighbourhood using indicators ranging

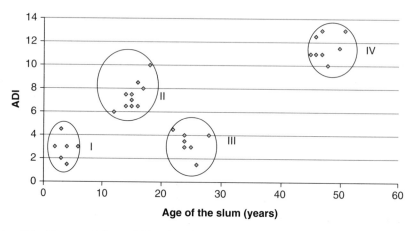

Figure 5.1 The age of slum neighbourhoods plotted against an aggregate development index

from the ways in which huts were constructed through to the kinds of pans households used for their cooking. The second indicator measured the quality of the built environment, counting the number of services available – water, toilets, legal and illegal electricity supplies, telephone connections, for instance – and their distance from the huts. The third indicator was an assessment of the cleanliness of the neighbourhood and included how well drained the area was, the presence of paving, whether garbage was collected, and if the local authority regularly controlled for mosquito infestation. With these measures formalised as rating scales, I went from area to area in the slum identifying what slum dwellers thought to be their neighbourhood, mapping these, and describing their demographic characteristics. I also asked about the history of each area. In all, I found 33 neighbourhoods and measured their development using the different measures of development we had designed. These variables I consolidated into an aggregate measure of development, which I plotted against the age of each neighbourhood. Figure 5.1 shows the results of this exercise.

As can be seen from Figure 5.1, the slum neighbourhoods clustered into four groups. Young underdeveloped slums and old developed slums tallied with the theory of development that had informed the exercise. But the slum neighbourhoods that were approximately between 15 and 25 years old appeared to be travelling along rather different trajectories of development.

Let me, for a moment, disaggregate one of the indexes to explain the next move. Each of the neighbourhoods may be described as a case in the research. The attributes used to understand the cases described traces of the reality of development in each. Take for instance the example of cooking pots. The expert community health workers explained that poor households will have a single battered and charcoal covered aluminium pan. At the other end of the scale, relatively well off households will display gleaming brass vessels. In between is a gradation of different numbers and kinds of pans, all of which are indicators of a household's poverty or relative wealth. For the health workers these pans describe very real social processes, through which they make acute judgements about the wealth and disposition of households. Or, put another way, the measurement of the type and number of pans is not transposed into a variable with independent causal powers, but describes traces of social systems as they are, should you have the expertise to decipher these attributes.

If I had treated my variables as independent (age of the slum) and dependent (aggregate development index) that were causally related, my next move in deciding who to sample would be to connect all the 33 points on the graph together, most likely through a method of log-linear regression. I would select a sample with reference to the line created. This I did not do. Instead, my sample was one slum from each of the clusters as is shown in Figure 5.1. I did this clustering exercise visually rather than mathematically. This approach assumed that I was investigating a complex social system with emergent causal properties, in which there was more than one way for the outcomes of development to be manifested. I went on to investigate the nature of the trajectories of development and what was causal in these trajectories.

I knew a great deal more about my sample as I set out to recruit women who lived in each of the four neighbourhoods and with whom I would go on to learn about development processes in the slum, through the lens of their experiences of health, descriptions of events of access to health providers, and their reasons for using these. At this early stage in the research, I was able to describe the relations of development in each of the neighbourhoods relative to others. This was achieved through bringing particular theories to bear on the research problem; these ideas precede method and technique including sampling choices and strategies.

Purposive work sets the scene for a programme of revision, elaboration, and reconstruction of theory. Getting out of the swamp, the uniquely important and under-reported purposive work of qualitative research provides the very foundations through which we purposefully choose information rich cases to be strategically compared in the research. It is these choices of cases that I consider in the next chapter.

6

PURPOSEFULLY CHOOSING CASES

In a realist sampling strategy cases provide bounded units in a potentially limitless open social system. They enable theorisation of contingent social processes; to test, refine, and elaborate ideas about what works for whom, in what circumstances, and why. Cases in qualitative research are most often presented as strong constructions, emergent or discovered from empirical enquiry. Their purpose is to describe what is going on in a particular setting. The first part of this chapter considers these case studies and how their construction leads to particular kinds of attempts at naturalistic, logical, or holographic generalisation. The analytic inductive strategies of intensive, exhaustive probing of individual cases and certain crucial types of cases are considered next, with their aim of identifying what a case is a case of. Closure of the case in this inductive strategy is essential to produce theoretical propositions. Casing is a realist methodological strategy in the research to challenge and re-specify received causal processes. It is used to work out the relationship between ideas and evidence. Casing purposefully works and reworks cases throughout the research. Interpretations and explanations are always provisional. This chapter discusses casing and presents three practical examples of casing, particularly in the early stages of research.

The constructed case study: 'What is going on here?'

The strongly constructed case collects together a specific object of study into a unique empirical system. According to Robert Stake (2008: 121) a case, or case study, is 'both a process of inquiry about the case and product of that inquiry'. This suggests the studied accumulation of empirical data, which allows the researcher to describe a particular activity or function within the context in which it is conceived to happen. This contextual account may, Stake suggests, include its historical background, physical setting, economic, political, and legal processes thought by the researcher and informants to impact on the activity and function.

A case developed in this way is the additive co-production and construction of empirical insight. Its purpose is to produce a descriptive unit that answers the question, often in considerable detail, what is going on here? The use of this case study does not, as Stake (2008) emphasises, have the purpose of theory building. Learning comes from the intrinsic study of the case, which in turn allows researchers to make naturalistic generalisations. Yvonna Lincoln and Egon Guba (1985: 120) describe this generalisation thus:

> if you want people to understand better than they otherwise might, provide them information in the form in which they usually experience it. They will be able, both tacitly and propositionally, to derive naturalistic generalizations that will prove to be useful extensions of their understanding.

For Lincoln and Guba the tacit knowledge evoked by a case study is important. Its rich, holistic, lifelike representation of the respondents' and researchers' co-constructions provides the reader with a vicarious experience of being there. Furthermore, through providing thick description, to use Clifford Geertz's (1973) term, of that which has been investigated and the context in which the case was collected, the reader can both probe for internal consistency and make judgements about the transferability of the case. The reader can evaluate and compare the case they are reading with a situation they know, as Patton (2002) suggested with logical generalisation in purposeful sampling strategies discussed in the second case in Chapter 2.

Lincoln and Guba (2007) go further in their elaboration of empirical insight towards a naturalistic generalisation. They draw on the metaphor of the hologram. The holographic image reproduces an object in three dimensions, its appearance varying depending on the perspective of the viewer. Under certain circumstances an observer can walk around the object, viewing it from back, front, and sides. For Lincoln and Guba this metaphor evokes the possibility of getting at the full information, should we know how to gain access. Filters of perspective can clarify the imperfect object. These, Lincoln and Guba suggest, are intrinsic to the holographic image. Faithfully recorded naturalistic data contains both filters and the imperfect object. The researchers' job is to draw out these insights from the empirical data in the image before them. This assumes our task in research is to carefully build constructions of reality from naturally occurring data, which are then re-described and re-presented in the technical language of social science. In their discussion of the sample and its relationship to naturalistic holographic generalisation this point is emphasised:

> Samples need not be representative in the usual statistical sense to render generalisation warrantable; any part or component is a 'perfect' sample in the sense that it contains all the information about the whole that one might ever hope to obtain. (Lincoln and Guba, 2007: 43 – emphasis in the original)

While qualitative samples cannot be representative in the statistical sense, it is the idea that perfection lies in the holographic image that is key in this view of the sample. For realists, however, the neglect of theory in this account limits the utility of a holographic metaphor. Richly descriptive cases of what is going on, the faithful rendering of co-produced cases that accumulate evidence, however faithfully, are limited by the assumption of the discovery, emergence, or construction of theory from the hologram.

All qualitative researchers will aim to produce descriptive accounts that have features of depth, thickness, and richness of account. The richly elaborated case that faithfully records empirical observation and provokes elaborate description about what is going on here is only one part of a casing strategy. This is the evidence derived from sampled units. As discussed in the previous chapter, realist cases are chosen for a very different reason – to test and refine theory. Cases are mutable, worked and reworked through continual interplay between evidence and ideas. The hologram, to pursue Lincoln and Guba's metaphor, is understood through informed judgement, not some intrinsic property of the image.

From the typical case to realist casing: 'What is this a case of?'

Robert Yin's account of analytic inductive case study research takes us closer to an understanding of the realist case. For Yin (2009: 38 – emphasis in the original):

> 'cases are not "sampling units" and should not be chosen for this reason. Rather individual case studies are to be selected as a laboratory investigator selects the topic of a new experiment.'

In the same way that a natural scientist will design an experiment to further insight into the phenomenon she is interested in investigating, so each case is selected because it can make a significant contribution to theory building and knowledge. Yin suggests that a case may be selected for three reasons. First, a case may be critical, it will confirm, challenge, or extend theory. Secondly, researchers may select a case because it is unique and provides an opportunity to document and analyse some one-off incident or process. Thirdly, the case may be representative or typical; it captures the circumstances and conditions of an everyday or commonplace situation and is informative about the average experience.

Here we are reminded of the theoretical or purposive sampling strategy described by Mason (2002) (see Chapter 3). Intellectual work and empirical contours are linked, sampling proceeds analytically and inductively through selecting cases to test theoretical propositions, account for rival explanations, and produce descriptive frameworks. Also inextricably bound up in the selection of the case and its subsequent analysis are the contextual conditions in relation to the case. But Yin (2009) advocates a much stronger experimental epistemology than that proposed in theoretical or purposive sampling strategies. He suggests that similar data are collected from each case in broadly the same way. A protocol should be drawn up to direct field investigation; this direction does echo the decisions to adopt sampling frames and derive quotas from these, as advocated by Mason (2002). Cases, Yin argues, should be selected through a logic of replication. Multiple cases are selected because the researchers predict there will be a similar result (a literal replication), or there will be 'contrasting results but for anticipatable reasons (a *theoretical replication*)' (Yin, 2009: 54 – emphasis in the original). This analytic induction is driven by cross case comparison, in which a rich theoretical framework states the conditions under which a particular phenomenon is likely to be found or not found; the selection of cases follows on from this framework.

Again, reminiscent of Mason's (2002) account of theoretical or purposive sampling strategies, this replication approach, as Yin (2009) emphasises, must be distinguished from the sampling logic of surveys. The purpose is not to sample a sub-set of an entire population or universe. The case study approach will not allow for claims to be made about the prevalence or frequency of a particular phenomenon. Instead, its purpose is to investigate particular topics in detail to test theory. This requirement for depth investigation within a rich theoretical framework means that researchers are constantly asking the question, 'what is this a case of?' In an analytic inductive strategy, as shown in Chapters 3 and 5, this question can eventually be answered in the research project because the boundaries of the case are closed. A universe is defined and the representativeness of the case can be established.

Casing

For realists, however, social systems remain open. It is notable that in the workshop that framed the book 'What is a case? Exploring the foundations of social enquiry' (Ragin and Becker, 1992), Howard Becker wanted to keep the question 'what is this a case of?' constantly open and never completely answered. The less certain a researcher is of the answer to this question, the better the research being done might be, Becker argued. The cases in research should be evaluated over and over again as the research progresses, the answer always tentative; a reflexive engagement between empirical data gathered in the research and the theories driving the research forward. As Charles Ragin (1992a: 6) argues '[w]orking through the relation of ideas to evidence answers [this] question'. The purposeful choice of cases can be neither a one-off selection made at the beginning of the research, nor will it stay the same throughout the research. For Ragin, the taxonomies of cases, data categories, theoretical categories, historically specific or substantive categories, to name but a few, give way to the use of cases as a research tactic which he calls casing. Casing is selectively invoked and re-invoked through the research by researchers to 'resolve difficult issues in linking ideas and evidence' (Ragin, 1992b: 217).

A realist approach does not take an agnostic stance towards theory. Theories (or ideas, to once again put it less grandly), not data points, are transferred between cases. Cases are chosen, formed, and reformed through the research with the purpose of testing and refining theory.

Transformation in a casing strategy

A realist purposeful sampling strategy builds a system of information rich cases through which sets of ideas can be judged. These are strategies for interpretation and explanation. Casing, to follow Ragin's lead, is a practical and methodological strategy in the research that allows for system building to be done. The choosing of cases is informed in the early research by the purposive work, through which the bold conjectures or presuppositions that inform the research are developed. As was discussed in the last chapter, these theories are constrained in particular ways by internal and external powers and liabilities. In the reflexive and interpretative engagement of purposive work, embryonic theories are constructed and propositional statements elaborated, which are nonetheless bold. These explain that which we seek to elaborate, test, and refine in the research. Units purposefully chosen in this system building are chosen and transformed as cases.

The basic ingredients of realist sampling are summarised in Figure 6.1. The choices about whom or what to sample (the regularity) purposefully proceeds through explaining context, mechanism, and outcome. In making choices we specify in some way what each or some of these are in our provisional account of the sample:

> This unit was chosen because it brings together this experience (regularity), in this particular setting (context), leading to this way in which we can see an expression of this social process (outcome), and we have an idea that these forces (mechanisms) are at play in producing this configuration.

This statement will be familiar to scientific realists and summarises a 'model of a stratified reality being composed generatively' (Pawson and Tilley, 1997: 72). Like Figure 6.1, it summarises the choices and capacities to purposefully sample units. The purposive work is represented by the left of the two eggs in the figure. In the early research, even with the wealth of insight brought to it through purposive work, the ideas upon which choices as to whom or what to

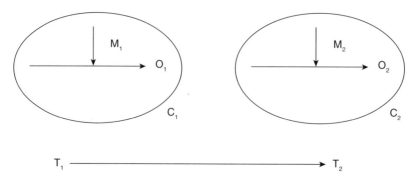

Figure 6.1 Transformative systems in realist sampling (after Pawson and Tilley, 1997: 73)

sample are simple, abstract, and incomplete (Ragin, 1992b), even naïve (Lakatos, 1976). These explanations of the cases in the research provide a conceptual scaffold to purposeful sampling. They offer support to the justifications for our choices in a way that a blank slate (*tabula rasa*) theoretical sampling strategy never can. Furthermore, it will not be long before these ideas are brought into direct engagement with empirical evidence in the research, providing opportunities to test ideas, account for context, and refine explanations, cause and outcome. The cases we choose will not be the same at the end of the research. They will be transformed as indicated by line T_1 to T_2 in Figure 6.1. 'New cases' as John Walton (1992: 127) observes, 'become strategic when they challenge or re-specify received causal processes'.

In the next chapter I argue that the sample is transformed through strategies of casing as the research progresses, as suggested in Figure 6.1, where $\{C_1, M_1, O_1\}$ is transformed to $\{C_2, M_2, O_2\}$. The remainder of this chapter considers the first configuration represented in the figure $\{C_1, M_1, O_1\}$. In early fieldwork abstract and incomplete insights from purposive work inform purposeful choices. In the next section I consider how these purposeful choices are made, returning once again to the slums of Mumbai.

Applying purposive work: the purposeful choice of a sample in a Mumbai slum

Discussed in the previous chapter is the purposive work that went into getting out of the swamp to provisionally understand a Mumbai slum. As noted, from this work four slum neighbourhoods were purposefully chosen because I thought these expressed the basic ingredients of realist explanation – context, mechanism, and outcome – in particular ways. These configurations are presented in Figure 6.2.

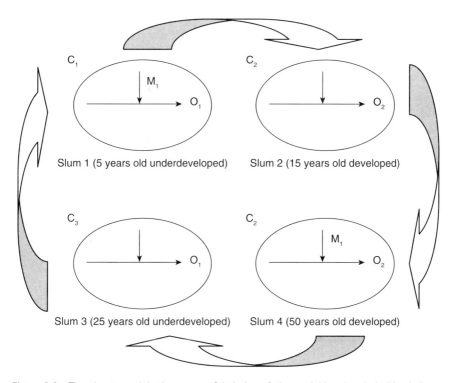

Figure 6.2 Theories to explain the purposeful choice of slum neighbourhoods in Mumbai

As this figure shows, three different contexts were purposefully chosen. As discussed above, defining contexts places ecological boundaries around that which is being investigated. These boundaries are neither physical, nor derived solely from some emergent property of data. They are mapped out conceptually through the interplay of ideas and empirical evidence.

In this example the early definitions of context derive from the survey in the slum. Context could be defined by geography. As part of the survey, participatory maps (see Emmel, 1998) were drawn by residents which demarcated the boundaries of a neighbourhood. For theoretical reasons these geographical boundaries were considered to be of little value. They were useful in mapping the slum as a whole, providing a descriptive patch-work-like map which triangulated the neighbourhoods (in the literal sense used by cartographers). The ideas that are described by C_1, C_2, and C_3 are accounts that combine ethnicity, religion, and caste. As in all purposeful strategies in realist sampling, experiences and events are brought into engagement with ideas. Some of these ideas are talked about by participants in which passing reference is made to broader social forces. In a

Mumbai slum, the name of a neighbourhood is important for instance, potentially capturing political, ethnic, religious, and caste allegiances in the urban political economy. It is the researchers responsibility to take these empirical observations and bring them into engagement with ideas; to propose mechanisms and to make choices to test and refine these powers and liabilities. The insiders' perspectives and the outsiders' understandings are mobilised to get at the traces of systems that make up reality.

Outcomes, in Figure 6.2 O_1 and O_2, also combine concept and empirical account. Here O_1 refers to an outcome of under-development, O_2 to relative development. As discussed in the previous chapter, they explain traces of reality understood through purposive work. Like the ages of the slums, they are stripped bare of the social processes that give them meaning. The research will elaborate these shallow accounts, giving them nuance, depth, and thick description and will explain causal powers and liabilities that account for the experiences of development in each of the neighbourhoods.

At this very early stage in the research, only one generative mechanism (M_1) is identified in Figure 6.2. This mechanism, it will be recalled from the discussion in Chapter 5, is the (somewhat deterministic) theory that one should see incremental improvement in development as the slum ages. It is derived from theories of epidemiological transition. Theoretically this mechanism makes sense in the youngest and oldest slum in the sample, but some other causal powers appear to be exerting their forces in Slums 3 and 4. The research is tasked with describing, elaborating, and explaining these causal accounts.

In this example, each of the four cases is a different configuration of context, mechanism, and outcome. Each is a tentative realist explanation that links ideas and evidence. These descriptions are only weak constructions and as such we should not be waylaid by acts of assigning evidence and ideas to context, mechanism, and outcome. Fruitless hours can be spent trying to work out if some part of this weak construction is context, or mechanism, or outcome. The effort is far better spent ensuring that evidence and ideas are adequately represented in the strongly interpretative account of the cases in the research. Each of these cases will be carried forward to offer direct support or rejection of theories. Together, the cases purposefully bring together bundles, configurations of ideas and evidence in a system built to compare, juxtapose, judge, and interpret these ideas.

Nuggets of insight: choosing cases purposefully

Often, as the example of research in a Mumbai slum shows, the insights upon which purposeful choices are made are far from robust. It is a matter of making do with whatever is available and using it creatively and to best advantage.

On other occasions, the resources available to researchers appear more sophisticated, providing opportunities to gain important insights towards making purposeful choices.

The purposive work through which purposeful sampling choices are made by Jane Elliott and colleagues (2010), for instance, rely on the UK National Child Development Study (NCDS), a large-scale longitudinal study started as the 1958 British birth cohort study. This was initially funded as a single wave perinatal mortality study with 17,000 children. Subsequent funding allowed for follow up surveys when the respondents were aged 7, 11, 16, 23, 33, 42, and 46 years.

These incredibly rich resources of longitudinal quantitative data allow Elliott and colleagues to do an analysis of the social mobility of the survey sample. Social mobility, they theorise, can be understood through the ways in which respondents move up, down, or stay stationary in the social hierarchy. Their method is to assign cohort members to one of three socio-economic groups – service class, intermediate class, and working class, dependent upon occupation. Using data on the occupation of the father (drawn from data collected when the respondents were 16 years old, or 11 years old if the information was missing in the later survey), and the respondent's occupation at 46 years old (or at 42 years old if this information was not recorded in the later survey), Elliott and colleagues classify each cohort member's socio-economic trajectory. Cohort members are assigned to one of four groups: 1) stable service class; 2) upwardly mobile into service class; 3) downwardly mobile from the service class; and 4) stable other (intermediate and working class). Through these analyses these authors have identified particular regularities as trajectories of change or sameness that characterise the cohort. The processes that lie beneath these trajectories remain hidden. But they provide a theoretical framework through which the sample can be purposefully sampled and cases chosen.

This early analysis from quantitative accounts can be even more detailed, as Elliott and colleagues go on to show. Also described is the way in which the sample is stratified using geodemographics. All 9,790 NCDS cohort members interviewed when they were age 50 years provided postcode information. From these data, the researchers were able to divide the cohort by three regions in the UK, and, less arbitrarily, by a much more detailed discriminator, Mosaic classification, which draws on over 400 variables to paint a rich picture of UK households in terms of socio-demographic profile, lifestyle, culture, and behaviour. Conducted using the 2006 edition of Mosaic, their analysis allowed for cohort members to be assigned to one of eleven groups, which range from 'symbols of success' through to those living in 'rural isolation'. Using these profiles, 238 cohort members were chosen to be interviewed in the qualitative research. These characteristics of the eventual sample are summarised in Table 6.1.

Table 6.1 Total number of qualitative interviews by social mobility and Mosaic profile drawn from cohort members of the age 50 years cohort of the NCDS (after Elliott et al., 2010: 26)

	Stable service	Upwardly mobile	Downwardly mobile	Stable other	All
1. Symbols of success	12	14	4	7	37
2. Happy families	2	12	8	6	28
3. Suburban comfort	6	11	2	12	31
4. Ties of community	3	8	3	9	23
5. Urban intelligence	1	3	3	2	9
6. Welfare borderline	0	0	2	3	5
7. Municipal dependency	0	1	1	3	5
8. Blue collar enterprise	0	6	4	6	16
9. Twilight subsistence	0	1	1	1	3
10. Grey perspectives	3	3	0	6	12
11. Rural isolation	1	2	0	6	9
Total number interviewed	28	61	28	61	178

Read one way, as Elliott and colleagues (2010) do, the row and column headings provide labels for the intellectual work and empirical contours, through which the cohort is stratified, and a theoretical target sample identified. They acknowledge that the term target sample is rarely used in qualitative research, but, note how useful this term is. It aims the sample at those who might be part of the response group.

Read through a realist sampling strategy, the column headings provide an early account to the research of context, while the rows, as discussed, provide a sense of the different regularities of social trajectory and constitute the early cases in the research. So, for instance, we can understand cohort members who fall into the stable service/symbol of the success group as being in a similar occupational group to their father, amongst the 10% wealthiest households in the country, and, somewhat intriguingly according to Experian (2006), commonly called Rupert and Felicity.

Quite how this private company that owns these data arrives at its typologies has, unfortunately to be taken on trust. The algorithms that manipulate the 400 or so variables are not published. Nonetheless, the reasoning for choices of cases can be explained, interpretations are made between the ideas and the evidence in the research.

The reasons for linking these cases to qualitative research are emphasised by Jane Elliott (1999: 101–102) elsewhere, where she notes that:

it is important not to lose sight of the individuals whose lives provide the data for the models. Although variables rather than individual people may become the subjects of the statistician's narrative, it is individuals rather than variables who have the capacity to act and reflect on society.

The qualitative research conducted with this target sample was concerned to understand how 'different individuals conceptualise social participation and the kinds of activities, which are meaningful to them' (Elliott et al., 2010: 9). Their questions are about process and comparison:

'why do some people remain consistently involved? Why do some people stop being involved? Why do some people start being involved?' (2010: 8–9)

They are bread-and-butter questions of qualitative researching. The purposive work preceding the purposeful selection of cases provides very little insight into these research questions. We understand nothing of the ways in which different individuals think about meaningful experiences of social participation, nor the events that are described through the ways in which they participate or exclude themselves socially. These, along with the generative mechanisms, the forces and liabilities that fire in a particular context to bring about a particular regularity of social participation and its outcome, will be explored, interpreted, and explained as the qualitative research progresses, and will be included in the working and reworking of cases in the acts of casing throughout the research. Nonetheless in the early research, this sophisticated purposive work using a large-scale quantitative longitudinal database and rather more opaque geodemographic resources, provides insight into context and regularities through which the sample is purposefully chosen.

The framing devices of a purposeful sample and the transformation of cases

The use of quantitative data to frame the purposeful choice of sample in qualitative research is widespread as the example from Elliott and colleagues' work above shows (see also Finch and Mason (1990) in Chapter 3, and Savage and colleagues (2005) in the previous chapter). In a further example, Robert Mackenzie and colleagues (2006), in research exploring the experiences of redundant steel workers at five steel plants in Wales, used a database maintained by the training arm of the workers' trade union, Steel Partnership Training. The dataset included all steelworkers made redundant between 2001 and 2003. The researchers drew a random sample of 125 workers, stratified by plant site, age, and occupation. In each of these cases, the purposive work that precedes the purposeful sampling choices provides very limited theorisation. The ways in which context, mechanism, and outcome can be described are constrained and any interpretations derived from these accounts of the sample are descriptive and abstract. These variables are stripped bear of the relationships, contexts, and powers that sustain them.

Nonetheless these cases, while using the limited insight of variables to make early choices, also exemplify the ways in which the limitations of these descriptors of the sample are overcome in the research.

Mackenzie and colleagues (2006) bring theoretical ideas into engagement with the empirical features of their sample, providing more expansive and explanatory accounts of those whom they sampled. Strategies are adopted to move from a superficial description to more sophisticated explanations of the sample, which are a synthesis of theoretical work and empirical evidence.

Gardiner and colleagues (2009: 132), draw a sub-sample from this larger sample of 125 redundant steel workers. As they note:

> the initial reading of the [125] transcripts [from interviews] revealed the diversity of individual responses to redundancy, and identified those individuals who were actively pursuing a new professional-type career. The transcripts of 18 of these 'career changers' who had provided the most detailed accounts [16 men and two women] were selected for further analysis ... Using [a] framework, a spectrum of career change experiences was identified.

For Gardiner and colleagues diversity is 'revealed' from the empirical evidence. Particular events and experiences are 'identified'. Unlike the sampling accounts from the quantitative research, however, these qualitative insights are much richer, nuanced, and 'detailed'. They are selected for this reason, but, as is common across the cases discussed here, these researchers bring evidence into engagement with theory in purposive work to produce a 'framework'.

This framework is an interpretation. The four dimensions to their framework – relational context, the cultural context, biographical experience, and the temporal dimensions of agency, each of which is further sub-divided into themes – have their roots in both the accounts of events and experiences of redundant Welsh steel workers and the intellectual work of the researchers. Gardiner and colleagues (2009: 731) note how important to their insight and understanding is Mustafa Emirbayer and Ann Mische's (1998) seminal paper, which discusses 'how forms of human agency interact with enabling and constraining contexts of action'. Theory always precedes empirical work.

This blurring of analysis, sampling, and ideas is a constant feature of any realist research. Gardiner and colleagues' work emphasises this blurring. The sample is chosen through the filter of extensive theoretically informed analysis that has gone before the choices made as to whom to sample. The (sub-) sample of 18 steel workers is drawn from the larger sample of 125. The description of its features is far more sophisticated. These researchers are able to describe their sample in considerable detail at a fairly early stage in the research. In common with many realist accounts, as I will show in the next chapter, they are able to produce a conceptual continuum and assign each of the 18 steel workers a position. Their continuum describes two poles of experience and a middling point:

Two are 'active career planners' – planning their career strategies before redundancy struck, using and being constrained by the services available through the plant employers and their union.

Ten are 'triggered career changers' – forced to consider new careers because of redundancy, and single minded in their pursuit of this new career, often facilitated by skill sets, supporting families, and their trade union.

Six are 'at a career crossroad' – unsure about whether to invest time and money in continuing to undertake training in another career after the unexpected bombshell of redundancy and significant uncertainty about whether they were on the right course because of commitments to family and income generation.

In this continuum the sample is richly elaborated through interpretation and explanation linking evidence and ideas. But, also being invoked here is a casing strategy. The subjects of study are no longer the 18 steel workers, but three cases, active career planners (who are Jeff and Derek), triggered career changers (represented by Robert and Terry), and at career crossroads (represented by Graham and Mike). These 'cases', as Gardiner and colleagues (2009: 733) note, 'illustrate the different sub-groups (to) better understand the interplay of structure, culture, biography and forms of agency in the experience of moving on from redundancy'.

Gardiner and colleagues' (2009) work starts with a framework of all steel-workers made redundant between 2001 and 2003 at five Welsh steel works, from which 125 were selected at random (Mackenzie et al., 2006). Of these 18 are selected for further investigation after considerable insight is gained into their experiences of redundancy. These are sub-divided down again into three cases to best account for the relationships between ideas and evidence in the research.

Conclusion

The way in which the sample is described changes as the research progresses. This happens in two quite distinct but interlinked ways. First, as each of the three cases in this chapter has shown; the account of the sample will be elaborated, bringing researchers' ideas into play with evidence to produce more sophisticated interpretations of cases. Secondly, casing, through linking ideas and evidence will purposefully configure and reconfigure, fuse and split the sample to better resolve these relationships.

The purpose of casing and of our sample is to test and refine theory. The strength of this strategy is that it happens in the research, intrinsic to the reflexive process of doing research. There is no ordained or prescribed process, rather the necessary conjunction of researchers' ideas and events and experiences recorded from real lives (from lively people to dusty documents), from purposive work to purposeful choices, drive forward interpretation and explanation. It is to this driver that I turn in the third part of this account of a realist sampling strategy.

7

INTERPRETATION AND EXPLANATION

Sampling choices cast short and long shadows through the research. Each choice, be it ideas and conjectures arising from purposive work to be tested and refined through the research, or a case purposefully chosen in an attempt to tackle these intellectual puzzles, will inform our next sampling choice in the research. These short shadows may inform another choice, a different context explained, refined theory to be tested in a new configuration or reconfiguration of cases. The longer shadows of the sample are cast forward to the claims we can make from the research. This chapter considers the ways in which the powers and liabilities acting on regularities of sampling in particular contexts lead to particular outputs. The possibilities, nature, and kind of access to particular individuals or groups, for instance, provide invaluable insight, as do investigations of innovative recruitment strategies including knocking on doors, snowballing, and ethical engagement with the sample and informed consent. Reflexive engagement with these practical considerations in the research emphasise the ever extending descriptive baseline, the impossibility of a representative sample, and the ways in which casing informs explanation and interpretation from the research.

Access and interpretation

Access to those researchers want to sample in research is most often assumed to be a practical problem. Some method or strategy is required through which sufficient trust and rapport is established to allow for research instruments to be successfully applied, data gathered, and research objectives met. Thinking rather differently, a realist account of sampling incorporates the very process through which units (or subjects) are accessed into its explanation. The research, as will be recalled from Chapter 4, is as much a social object as the phenomena being investigated. Reflexive engagements with these processes of access provide theoretical insight into the relationships between researchers and researched, including into social and institutional norms, values, and inter-relationships within which access to the units of enquiry is made possible. Access, whether successful or not, to those with whom we wish to conduct research provides insight into relationships through which potential participants in the research consider it worthwhile or otherwise to be included. Reflection on these processes cast light on the reasons for the judgements they make. Process of access, like all powers and liabilities, add to description, interpretation, and explanation.

Trust is so often mobilised as key to access and successful research. As Martyn Hammersley and Anna Traianou (2012: 15) observe, a researcher's personal attributes of trustworthiness are very widely valued. These are of 'considerable significance in many of the contexts in which qualitative researchers carry out their work, especially given that the researcher often enters as a stranger'. It is the act of making researchers un-strange to potential participants in research that a considerable part of the literature on access focusses (Emmel et al., 2007). Less well considered are the dimensions of building a trustful relationship; the ways in which researchers think they can build a trustful engagement with their proposed sample and the insights these empirical encounters give us into the subjects in the research.

As a brief example, Tom Clark (2008) has considered the ways in which research is hampered by participants' unwillingness to engage in research because they feel over-researched. Through interviewing qualitative researchers, Clark learned that the most common symptom of over-research is fatigue with the research process. He observes that it is not just researchers who actively negotiate and manage research encounters. Participants have their own perceptions of engagement, which they too manage and negotiate. A likely reason for research fatigue, and subsequent withdrawal or refusal to be involved in research is, according to Clark (2008: 953) where participants perceive that 'repeated engagements do not lead to any experience of change or where the engagement comes into conflict with the primary aims and interests of the research(ed) group'.

Participants' aims and interests may relate to practical concerns, their time and other resources. These can most times be addressed in practical ways, such as through payment and negotiation to be involved in the research. But, as importantly and often neglected, participants have theories about the phenomenon under investigation; how it should be interpreted, explained, and addressed. If the research fails to consider these mechanisms then participants may feel there is little point in being involved in the research. Research fatigue inevitably follows. Addressing mechanisms is not, I suggest, necessarily about positioning research as participatory action research at the vanguard of change.

Most research does not have emancipatory aims, its objectives focus on generating new knowledge into a social phenomenon. The reason we choose subjects in particular contexts to be involved in research is because they provide insights into events and experiences we are concerned to investigate, interpret, and explain. The ways in which participants describe how they are able to act and the options available to them are a result of the working and reworking of narratives about a phenomenon through particular sets of ideas. These ideas are, in turn, constrained by the material setting and cultural meanings of social practice available to them. Participants have, nonetheless, aims and interests they consider are legitimate. These must be considered and addressed in some way in the research for access to be successful.

It is through recognising that access is a process managed and maintained through negotiation that we gain considerable practical and theoretical insight into the sample in the research. Trustworthiness can neither be reified to a number of features a researcher should have, nor be built through applying a range of tools or techniques. It is an account of the relational features through which participants feel it is safe to allow researchers access to their lives, including the ways in which participants feel the research is relevant to them. These powers and liabilities contribute in significant ways to interpretation and explanation from the research.

Accessing people like us

It is, I contend, because research is made possible through relationships between researchers and participants, that a considerable part of qualitative researching is done with people like us. This observation is anecdotal, my gut feeling, but one that holds considerable sway in any review of qualitative research. Returning to Elliott and colleagues' (2010) study discussed in the last chapter, it will be recalled that the target sample was identified through an analysis of NCDS large-scale quantitative longitudinal survey and Mosaic profiles. As Table 6.1 shows, target samples in each cell of the matrix are representative of the NCDS cohort. After successful interviews were conducted, the achieved sample was compared with the target. This rare opportunity provides insight into the characteristics of those who chose not be involved in the research, or were for some other reason hard to reach. Interviews were conducted with 71% of the target of 238 cohort members. Forty declined to be interviewed; 17 said they were too busy; 13 refused, citing other reasons such as family illness; 6 felt they were being asked to be interviewed too soon after the previous census interview; and 4 cancelled the interview and the interviewer was unable to make further contact.

These kinds of insight are available to most researchers tracking their successful or unsuccessful access in recruitment strategies. But given that the researchers had much more descriptive insight of the target sample from the longitudinal survey data and Mosaic profiles than most qualitative researchers, they are able to do analysis and say a great deal more than usual. They show, for instance, that men were significantly more likely than women to participate (1.86:1, p=0.014). Men were slightly more likely to agree to be interviewed regardless of employment status. Women were more likely to agree to an interview if they were in part-time work. Women who had not voted in the 2001 General Election had a higher refusal rate, as did both men and women who were cohabiting and who self-reported poor to fair health. Added to this, the methods used allowed Elliott and colleagues to identify selection bias in the sample. In the NCDS cohort at age 50 years, 34.9% had a degree or higher qualification, the proportion in the qualitative sample was 42.2%. The 'sample of qualitative interviews was somewhat biased towards those who reported voting in the last general election ... were better educated ... with better self-reported health'. This analysis of participation 'suggests that social participation levels among those interviewed were likely to be somewhat higher than among the cohort as a whole' Elliott and colleagues (2010: 38) report.

There is something rather intriguing here, which reverberates across many qualitative samples. The characteristics Jane Elliott and colleagues describe in the sample they accessed – healthy, better educated, active participants in society – are characteristics one might ascribe to university researchers. Those who chose to be involved in the research hold a homology of position, a social proximity and familiarity with researchers and research, to use Pierre Bourdieu's description. Bourdieu (2002) coined the idea in extensive research to understand social suffering in contemporary society, and also to explain the relationships that are possible between researcher and participants. Homologies of position lead to what Bourdieu (2002) describes as 'non-violent' relationships in the interview; a level playing field of social and linguistic capitals.

A further way of investigating the ways in which samples are constituted in research is to review the research and archives of other social scientists in their historical context, as Mike Savage (2010) has done. In his review of research in the 1950s he observes a bias in samples. Elizabeth Bott and Jim Robb's study of families, discussed in the previous chapter, for instance, is not a representative sample in any way 'but one which was elicited through their interest in research and indeed the social sciences' (Savage, 2010: 80). Most of the subjects were young, metropolitan, educated, held left-wing values and, according to Savage's reading of Bott and Robb's field notes, were 'committed to the value of social scientific research in what they saw as a rationally planned welfare state ... the sample itself presented to the researchers because they were attracted by the very idea of being researched' (2010: 10). The researchers' and their sample held similar outlooks, views, and ideas, grounded in similar norms, and experiences. Where they did not have these similarities, as in the case of a working class family whose baby had just died, Bott's co-researcher, Robb, describes how he feels like he is regarded as a bit of a fraud. He talks of 'my usual difficulty with working class families that I was always conscious of and uncomfortable about the difference between my standards and theirs …' (Robb cited in Savage, 2010: 9), a difference of experience which, Savage observes, leads to a distance forming between researchers and respondents and the setting of boundaries, despite Robb's strategy of building rapport with household members through treating them as potential friends.

Historical evaluation can reveal the homologies and dissimilarities of position between the chosen sample and researchers. So too can reflection by researchers. When Andrew Clark and I (with Frances Hodgson) set out to investigate Connected Lives in a mixed residence urban area (see Chapter 4) our purposive work led us to purposefully sample four groups between the ages of 18 and 26 years: university students; young professionals; long-term residents living in less affluent circumstances; and ethnic minority groups. Looking back through our field notes, access to university students and young professionals, who were characteristically in graduate jobs, was quicker and much easier than for the other two groups. It demanded much less negotiation because there was an implicit understanding as to the nature of the research and why we were interested to generate knowledge about how best to investigate networks, neighbourhoods, and communities using qualitatively driven mixed methods (see Emmel and Clark, 2009). Trust, and therefore access, was quickly established through our homologous positions. For the other two groups, there was considerable negotiation and the building of relationships of trust using the methods of access described by Emmel and colleagues (2007).

I am unable to substantiate my earlier observation that homologies of position between researchers and samples dominate in qualitative researching because historical accounts are limited. The observations from Connected Lives are, like Savage's interpretation of Elizabeth Bott's research, drawn from scrutiny of unpublished field diaries. This is significant, because within these unpublished sources lie the presuppositions and insights that describe many features of our sample understood through the work done to access and recruit them to the study.

Most often, however, samples are described in much more rudimentary terms, mistaking the language about what we know and describe of the samples' existence for what exists (Scambler, 2013), the linguistic fallacy discussed in Chapter 4. Lack of space, alongside conventions in reporting research, are likely reasons for these variable driven descriptions of the sample. These accounts of the sample might as well be describing a sack of potatoes. We are told their weights and measures, but how they got into the sack, how they were organised, we shall never know.

Accessing people unlike us

There are exceptions in which researchers report relational features of their sample in considerable detail. These are research projects that specifically choose to access hard-to-reach individuals and groups. An investigation of methods of access to these cases points to the ways in which the descriptive baseline of the sample in research is extended. Accounts of access to hard-to-reach groups also undergird the observation made in the previous section: we most often tend to do research with people like us.

Susan Ostrander (1993: 7 – emphasis in the original), who conducts research with elite groups, observes that 'social scientists too rarely "study up"'. While Rist (1981: 272 – emphasis in the original), observes that research is rare with marginalised and vulnerable groups because 'allowing *outsiders* to come in is risky'. The emphasis each of these authors chooses to apply is telling. Regardless of whether those we choose to sample are in the left or the right tails of a (Pareto) distribution of power/wealth/capitals they are unlike researchers. A reflexive engagement with the ways in which they are different from us and similar to each other is a necessary part of access. But more than this, the insights of access are necessary parts of the interpretation of the sample.

Harriet Zuckerman's account of access to Nobel Laureates in science in the United States fascinates at two levels: first, through the ways in which she built trust, and secondly the ways in which her participants, an ultra-elite who occupy the topmost strata of science, frame the possibilities in the research through their relationship with the researcher. As one Nobel chemist remarks:

> I said to myself before you came, "If she wants to ask me about social things, I will get her out of here fast". But you asked me about important things … (Zuckerman, 1972: 165).

Like Nobel Laureates, evaluation of the importance of the research is central in access to individuals and groups who populate the other pole of a continuum of hard-to-reach individuals and groups. These people are often characterised as poor, powerless, vulnerable, and marginalised. Yet, they too make assessment of whether the research addresses their real aims and interests. They may, as Emmel and colleagues (2007) have shown in a discussion of access to socially excluded individuals and groups, rely for that judgement on gatekeepers they trust. Or researchers may adopt a range of strategies, such as peer interviewers, immersion in communities, and snowballing towards generating trust and access to hard-to-reach individuals and groups.

Whatever the social and institutional norms, values, and inter-relationships of the group with whom the research is being undertaken, researchers will have to understand why and how these make them hard to reach. They will need to explore and account for these mechanisms in their processes of access. As an example, with marginal and vulnerable groups it might be absolutely inappropriate to provide information sheets or demand written and signed consent, for instance (see Emmel et al., 2007). While with an elite, like those who participate in charitable foundations in Boston, Massachusetts (Ostrander, 1993), information about each aspect of the research encounter in a written form will be absolutely expected.

Strategic choices to build and maintain relationships with hard-to-reach individuals and groups arise from insight in the research and an understanding of the sample. This insight is extended in the research through interaction. We seek to maintain trustworthiness, credibility, and rapport through empathy and ongoing reflection. An appropriate response demonstrates our probity and commitment to those with whom we are doing research and allows for ongoing access. As I have also shown, participants engage in research because they think it is worthwhile to them. As researchers we are obliged to reflexively engage with and understand mechanisms; what our sample are willing to discuss with us and why they think it is important.

Answering questions like these are perhaps easier when conducting research with people who are unlike us, often described as hard to reach. There is contrast between experiences of social and institutional norms, and ideas. Practices of access and maintaining a sample are mechanisms, powers and liabilities, which fire in particular contexts. Explaining these powers within which access is gained are essential elements in extending the descriptive baseline of the cases in the research.

An ever-extending descriptive baseline and the impossibility of a representative sample

As noted in Chapter 5, in an analytic inductive approach the representativeness of the sample is not known at the outset, the universe is explained as the research progresses. This view of representativeness in research is quite different from what Mason (2002) describes as the representative logic of quantitative research. These approaches are linked, however. Both assume that social systems are closed by our descriptions of them. As an example, insights gained through practices of access once again bring into question the appropriateness of variable-centric accounts of the sample, and by extension bring into question claims that a particular sample is representative of something or someone. The representative sample is a product of the application of quantitative sampling theory, in which every member of a pre-defined population has an equal chance of selection. This is a long-established and hard-fought-for axiom, best summed up in the opinion poll market research technologies developed in the early twentieth century. For George Gallup, one of the pioneers of the opinion poll method, the representative sample pertains:

> If a sample is accurately selected, it represents a near replica of the entire population. It is a miniature electorate with the same propor- tion of farmers, doctors, lawyers, Catholics, Protestants, old people, young people, businessmen, laborers and so on, as is found in the entire population. (Gallup, 1944: 21)

Such a view of the representative sample hinges on an assumption that any population may be defined and is finite. This view of representativeness is essential to the opinion poll, in which Gallup sought to represent a nation. Even when the sample appears unrepresentative, it is in fact representing something in the eye of the beholder. Gallup's samples would, as Thomas Osbourne and Nikolas Rose (1999) note, less than adequately represent women, Black Americans, and the lower social classes. But Gallup (1944) could justify this choice; the sample represented a particular population. As Gallup (1944: 28) observes 'in a number of southern states, many poor people do not vote because of the poll tax … the great majority of Negroes are in effect disenfranchised'. This is purposive work by researchers that leads to a definition of a population from which a quota sample is drawn. The sample's claim to be representative rests on this prior plan, a simulacrum of the population, from which decisions are made to interview pre- determined individuals selected with regard to particular factors. In Gallup's case these included age, sex, political affiliation, place of residence, socio- economic status, and race, amongst others. A representative sample relies, to use C. Wright Mills' (1959: 215) summary of the axiom, on 'that horrible little phrase about "knowing the universe before you sample it"'.

For realist researchers this simulacrum of the population is weak; for while it has the form or appearance of the population, it does not possess its substance or proper qualities. It is a mere guide, a framework that will be elaborated in considerable detail as the research progresses. As Pawson and Tilley (1997: 120 emphasis in the original) observe, 'the very notion of 'representativeness' or 'typicality' of a case gets utterly lost as the descrip- tive baselines increase' in the research. The way in which cases are described, interpreted, and explained in the research will change. Relationships between evidence, ideas, and practices of researching will be resolved. And furthermore, although these properties do not fall out of the data, the dynamic and contingent nature of that which is being investigated must be considered; the sample are subjects in process. Whatever we choose to sam- ple existed before we sampled them and our understanding of them changes in the research. These temporal considerations have implications for inter- pretation and explanation through the resolution of evidence, ideas, and practice. These considerations are investigated here through two methods, the first explores what happens when a researcher knocks in an arbitrary way on doors along a street, second is the more familiar snowball method.

Door knocking: from ideas to evidence to ideas

Tacit knowledge and arbitrary decisions are frequent in research, whether we want to admit to them or not. Our ability to categorise is an important one, but the researcher's skills to disrupt, question, and re-describe categories is essential. Katherine Davies (2011) describes how she set out to recruit individuals living in households in a northern English city to a study of family resemblances. Her strategy was to knock on people's doors and ask them to be involved in the research. Her choice of which door to knock at was not capricious but carefully considered through purposive work, which included both tacit knowledge and an investigation of available evidence. Bringing hunches and evidence together allows for choices to be made about whom to sample, and also for the testing and refining of theories about the sample.

With her co-researchers, she chose a number of streets in two areas of the city called Finlay Edge and Harnsworth. The choice was based on impressions of the areas from driving through them in a car. Finlay Edge, they categorised as typically working class, made up of red brick terraced houses with front doors opening out onto the street. Harmsworth is more middle class, with semi-detached houses and well kept gardens. Behind the doors of the houses in both these areas lived families, the researchers thought. To establish the make-up of households and test the tacit assumptions made in their choices, small area statistics derived from census data aggregated to about 120 households were collected and interpreted. These, Davies notes, confirmed some of her assumptions about the two areas, but also provided new and unexpected insights, particularly into the ethnic make-up of each neighbourhood.

Based on this purposive work Davies set to work walking the streets and knocking on doors. She emphasises the ethnographic potential of her chosen method. How through walking along her chosen streets she was able to complicate her initial generalised conceptualisations of the two areas. She notes subtle differences in the area, in the state of repair of houses and the care with which households in some streets tended their gardens. The experience of walking the street was an embodied experience in which sights, sounds, smells, and the feel of the pavement beneath her feet became important towards understanding the areas in which she was recruiting participants to her research. The categories gleaned from small area statistics were interpreted and reinterpreted as she began to appreciate the nuanced diversity she encountered in her walks and recorded in her field diary. Furthermore, as she recruited participants and did interviews with them she learnt more about the areas and the lives of residents in these areas. The research was not about community, but about the social significance of resemblances in families, be these 'looks, mannerisms, health, attributes, or talents, as examples' (Davies, 2011: 2). But through understanding the environments in which people lived and the diversity of these environments, even within a few streets, Davies was able to provide a depth of understanding that questioned stereotypes of what the people who lived in these areas are like. Categorical accounts that may have described her sample and guided her analysis of working class and middle class were challenged. The meanings and observations were enriched through their thick description. Recruitment, as a practice of researching becomes, Davies (2011: 10) notes, 'more than a means of producing a required sample'. New meaning of the places in which her participants lived was created that ensured that they were not displaced from their physical and social environment.

Furthermore, Davies shows how the method of recruitment through door knocking framed her understanding of the ways in which families conduct their family life in neighbourhoods, which then provided insight that was important towards interpreting the interview data she collected. Through walking the streets she not only gained insight into the places she was walking through, but also witnessed 'public performance of family enacted on the street' (2011: 9) such as a mother telling off her child, or someone calling a dog. These data collected during the practices of recruitment of the sample are insights that enrich, thicken, and add to empirical evidence collected in other ways, through interviews, focus groups, or even formal participant or non-participant observation. The sample casts off its thin and inadequate categorical descriptions. Furthermore, presuppositions, hunches, tacit knowledge, and conjectures researchers use to make choices are tested, refined, and even discarded as the research progresses. These are replaced with rich, diverse, and complex accounts of cases that contribute to interpretation and explanation. This does not mean that the sample becomes richer, necessarily, but our accreted description, interpretation, and explanation does. Katherine Davies' approach to door knocking is innovative. The principles of resolving the relations between evidence, ideas, and practice inform this innovation. In the next section different approaches to snowball sampling are considered. Contrasting quite different approaches emphasise the ways in which method, evidence, and ideas constantly interplay in developing interpretation and explanation.

Snowballs, chains, and networks: extending the descriptive baseline of the cases

Snowball sampling methods provide a method for recruitment of participants to the research through our ability to access particular networks with whom we have a relationship. These relationships may be built on friendship (Browne, 2005), getting to know a group through a key informant (Smith, 2005), or the shared experiences of a phenomenon that allow for initial access (Edwards et al., 1999). Howsoever the access starts, snowball sampling, otherwise referred to as chain sampling or network sampling, draws on this range of metaphors to describe a process of referral from one participant to the next in the research.

These metaphors point to slightly different features of the approach. Like a chain, there are clear and distinct links between the participants, as they are referred to researchers by previous participants. Like a network, the relationships between participants can be made explicit in the recruitment process, so we can gain insight into who is being recruited to the research and why they have been referred. And, in common with the way we might make a snowball, starting from a small handful of snow and rolling it along the ground until we have a ball sufficiently large enough to form the body of a snowman, we will collect some snow, but leave other snow behind. Similarly, as a method of recruitment, we will collect some participants to the research, but exclude others. A key feature of this strategy noted by most who have reported on it is that it gives access to participants with similar features.

How the methods of linked recruitment include particular individuals is a key consideration in deciding to use a snowball sample. It relies on the existence of shared characteristics that are recognised between the participants as bounding them meaningfully into a network. Most often these networks are exclusive. An investigation of sexuality amongst non-heterosexual women by Kath Browne (2005), for instance, recognises from the outset that this phenomenon may be considered to be outside the public realm. Her strategy to access insight to these private and hidden accounts is to use friendship networks to recruit women to her study. The initial link is the researcher herself, who is white, non-heterosexual, young (22–23 years old), and lives in a small town in the UK. As Browne (2005: 52) observes, this was 'central to the formation of my sample'. Using a snowballing strategy creates particular kinds of inclusion and therefore excludes others from the research.

Browne reflects on how a snowball approach excludes individuals that would not usually be part of her network, because of her age, ethnicity, and where she lives. Thus she observes that:

> Social settings (such as straight and gay pubs and nightclubs) were important spaces in which to meet friends and acquaintances who became participants in my research … (these) are predominantly white despite the ethnic diversity of the city. (Browne, 2005: 52)

But furthermore, some participants either did not wish to be part of the research or felt constrained in what they could discuss in the research because of the intimate relationships within the network upon which the sampling strategy relied. One participant, a friend of a friend, refused to be involved because she did not wish to divulge intimate details about her sex life to Browne. In contrast, the friendship networks in the research facilitated comfortable discussions among the participants about some aspects of their private lives and, as Browne points out, these friendships were important in facilitating certain kinds of conversations that may not have happened between strangers. However, some areas were still considered to be beyond the limits of acceptable conversation, including particular relationship dynamics between partners, for instance. In these situations the researcher is drawn into the participants' boundaries and alliances and somehow needs to make sense of these.

This notion of boundaries Browne (2005) draws from the work of Rosalind Edwards and colleagues' (1999) investigation of step-families. At the time of the research the step family was a very new concept (Edwards personal communication). Here these researchers consider the implications of the ways in which they might draw boundaries around a set of relationships that constitute a step-family. They speculate that many characteristics could be used including, for instance, biological and/or step-parents' marital status and childrens' residence, access patterns, and legal and administrative definitions. They point to the seemingly endless ways in which the step-family might be configured and reconfigured. What is more, they note that step-families describe and construct their family life. For Edwards and colleagues (1999), this presents a challenge, the ways in which researchers construct the boundaries of step-family may or may not fit with participants' constructions. This agreement or disagreement with researcher-imposed categories will, in turn, lead to a willingness or resistance to participate in the research. An issue they felt was particularly important because their snowball recruitment strategy proceeded through contacting one member of a step-cluster (family), who was usually the biological or step-mother, and then seeking to interview further members of the step-cluster.

Their use of the term step-cluster reflects Edwards and colleagues' reluctance to impose their constructions of step-family. Indeed, they sought to make the boundaries of the categories that define the sample as porous as possible. As an example, when addressing the tension (to use their term) present when debating at what point childrearing comes to an end, Edwards et al. (1999: 22) observe that:

> Being a parent (and being a child of your parent/s) does not end at a particular age or stage, but 'childrearing' can be more circumscribed. … We decided against drawing a fixed boundary in terms of an upper age limit for children of the separated or divorced parents within our step-cluster.

This strategy of co-construction is a technique to avoid posing a theory in the research: producing an idea about what might happen for a step-family in some particular circumstance and experiences of rearing children. There are no ideas to test, refine, revise, or adjudicate between. No context is mobilised to frame this work beyond the micro-sociology of each family investigated. Instead, what is advocated is a co-construction of the terms in the research. The subjects in the research define the ways in which they wish to be categorised, with a gentle nudge from the researchers. A blank slate (*tabula rasa*), in which the researchers provide the slate and chalk and the participants write a script. For Edwards and colleagues (1999), strong co-constructions lead to the dissolution of power relationships between researchers and participants. The unwillingness to categorise a sample and then recognise the fallibility of these categories in the research leads, potentially, into a relativist wormhole in which each co-construction is yet another descriptive account lacking in explanatory causal power.

Now, for realists, the best we can say of these constructions is that they raise consciousness about that which is the focus of study. In returning to Kath Browne's study discussed earlier in this section, she takes a rather different tack in her investigation of sexuality amongst gay women. She accepts that the relationship she has with her sample is as both friend and researcher. She is always in some position or relation to the sample. As researcher she reflexively engages with both the process of access to individuals and their insights into events and experiences. Her interpretation of the salient features of the relationships between researcher and participant, and between participants in this snowball sampling strategy, are accounts of social and institutional norms, values, inter-relationships, and culture which find their expression in the ways in which those recruited are involved in the research.

That meanings of networks are real and have powers and liabilities guides David Smith (2005) in his application of a snowball sampling strategy to recruit participants to an investigation of social exclusion and the informal economy in a London social housing estate. The starting point of this chain sampling strategy is the brother of a school friend, notorious on the estate for his drug dealing and reputation for larceny. As Smith (2005: 13) observes, '[m]y interest in Steve was not in his drug dealing but in his wide array of contacts … ' Through Steve, Smith gains access to key informants who provide him with particular and informed insights into the informal economy and experience of lone-parenting on the estates, and at the same time refer him to further participants with similar experiences. Snowball sampling facilitates referral of the researcher from individual to individual along a chain. These are networks of distribution and exchange, in which material goods and shared accounts of events and experiences in particular contexts are linked directly to meanings, beliefs, motives, and ideology. The interpretation of the participants' accounts are always:

> Influenced both by the material circumstances in which they exist and by the cultural resources that provide actors with ways of making sense of their situations (Maxwell, 2012: 21).

It is the similarities of context and accounts of events and experiences within his sample that Smith emphasises. He notes that '[s]nowball sampling involves sampling within rather than across cases. As a consequence it tends to promote a sample that is homogeneous in its attributes, rather than providing linkages to groups where social characteristics are different' (Smith, 2005: 14). This is the strength of the strategy of using a snowball sample. It provides experience in a concentrated form: a small handful of individuals with a deep and intense knowledge through their inclusion in the material and cultural formations of particular actions (see Ken Plummer, 1983: 101).

The narrowness of the accounts obtained through a snowball/chain/network sampling strategy points to the challenge in the claims that can be made. Interpretation and explanations cannot be read off the data, they are mediated through researchers' theory and insight. These are not strongly co-constructed accounts, but weak constructions and strong interpretations and explanations. They seek to get at real accounts, however fallible and open to further interrogation.

There is a strong tendency, for instance, to over-emphasise the strength of the informal economy in low-income communities, as David Smith points out. A few families apparently living beyond their means, and a handful of well known individuals on an estate with the skills to mend cars, become indicators of the extent of unpaid work. Political campaigns and media hyperbole on an issue like welfare benefit fraud 'feed into residents' common-sense perceptions to confirm their beliefs that abuse of the system is widespread' (Smith, 2005: 145). Events and experiences are confirmed for individuals in the research and, subsequently generalised to contexts. The researchers' challenge is to take these perspectives, understand how they interact with and are limited by the situations in which they are reported, and bring sets of theoretical presuppositions to the situated character of knowledge.

Snowball/chain/network sampling strategies are a strategic choice to access participants and build a sample in research. Inherent in the choice are powers and liabilities – for a snowball sample, providing access to rich accounts of networks, while being limited by the focus of links along the chain. It is, in this way, like any strategy we may choose to use to access participants in research. Context, process (or regularity), and participants' and researchers' ideas continuously engage with accounts of events and experiences. They accrete towards interpretation and explanation made possible within the capacities of the research.

Conclusion

Practices, theory, and evidence are in continual engagement in interpreting and reinterpreting the sample. When brought together through a casing methodology, evidence and practices are interpreted and explained alongside each other. The sample's extended descriptive baseline becomes essential insight towards adjudicating between ideas and testing and refining these. As researchers we take insights about what we consider the characteristics and causal powers of our sample to be. We argue and debate our models and heuristics within our research teams (Greenhalgh et al., 2009), and in wider academic communities. The outcomes of these processes of adjudication are ideas that make claims about what works for whom and in what contexts and why.

In common with the discussions about access, door knocking, and snowball sampling discussed in this chapter, ethical practices are interpreted in light of particular situations. For the American Anthropological Association (1998), for instance, processes of informed consent are dynamic and continuous. They should be initiated in project design and continue through implementation by way of dialogue and negotiation with those studied. The relationships researchers develop with participants are likely to be close and enduring. It is an essential element of research practice that the limits of relationships are carefully and respectfully negotiated. These negotiated ethics are situated in practice. Reflecting the discussion in this chapter about how engagement with a sample in research happens, ethical practices require 'reflexive judgements about the whole situation in which action is taking place, including the identities of researcher and researched, and the forces, of various kinds, operating upon and within this situation' (Hammersley and Traianou, 2012: 33–34). Emphasised here, in what is for these authors a radical turn in interpreting ethics and ethical practice, is the "value-rich' rather than 'value-neutral' character of social research' (2012: 33 emphasis in the original). While recognising that transparent reflexivity of the 'whole' is not possible (see Chapter 4), we must however, do the best we can to account for and explain the practices, evidence, and ideas brought together in explanation and interpretation in the research.

Also emphasised in this chapter is the absolute lack of rules, tools, and procedures to propel forward casing strategies. Relational, processual, and reflexive analysis between practice, ideas, and evidence are intrinsic to the interpretative power of realist research. These principles are often considered unpredictable by external powers to the research. I have touched on one area of a realist qualitative method that presents challenges to external powers because of the lack of pre-established procedure in the final part of this chapter, ethical practice. In the next chapter I address another challenge to many research governance structures – sample size.

8

SAMPLE SIZE

This chapter considers one of the most frequently asked questions, how big (or small) does a sample have to be in qualitative research? I consider the key arguments for sample size in the three sampling strategies of theoretical sampling, purposeful sampling, and theoretical or purposive sampling considered in the first part of the book. I also deal with the practical problem of sample size in qualitative research, which is given little attention in many methodological accounts. The realist sampling strategy considers the ways in which fragments of insight are collected in qualitative research. To ask how big the sample size is or how many interviews are enough is to pose the wrong question. It is far more useful to show the ways in which the working and reworking of relationships between ideas and evidence in the research are a foundation for the claims made from the research.

Large numbers, small samples, cases

Even studies with apparently large sample sizes are small in qualitative research. The largest qualitative samples do not seem to exceed about 200 units. Savage and colleagues' (2005) sample size of 186 participants and Alan Wolfe's (1996) study with 200 interviewees in the US investigating the experience of being middle class are typical. But even with an apparently large headline number of participants these samples are really rather small. To appreciate how small we need to consider how each sample is divided down. As will be recalled from the discussion in Chapters 5 and 6, Savage and colleagues' sample was sub-divided across four residential areas in Manchester's suburbs; in Wilmslow, 44 participants were recruited (population 30,326), in Cheadle, 43 (population 12,158), in Chorlton, 47 (population 13,512), and in Ramsbottom, 47 household members answered the researchers' questions (population 14,635). Similarly, Wolfe's investigation was in four cities from across the four corners of the United States, in which two areas were selected. Twenty-five individuals were sampled from eight areas; on the East Coast, Boston (Brookline, Massachusetts population 58,732 and Medford, Massachusetts, population 56,173); in the South, Atlanta (Southeast DeKalb County, Georgia, population 691,893 and Cobb County, Georgia, population 701,325); in the Midwest, Tulsa (Broken Arrow, Oklahoma, population

98,850 and Sand Springs, Oklahoma, population 18,906); and on the West Coast in San Diego (Eastlake, California, population 243,916 and Rancho Bernardo, California, population 49,115).

As Wolfe (1998) notes, in a CBS News/New York Times poll conducted in 1992, 75% of respondents considered themselves middle class when asked a question: 'When presidential candidates talk about the middle class, do they mean people like you?'. That is 194,938,941 people using the US Census Bureau's National Intercensal Estimates (1990–2000). Both Wolfe's and Savage and colleagues' samples on superficial inspection give the impression of big numbers, but when examined carefully even these relatively large studies are the slightest incursion into the populations investigated.

But these numbers are merely a distraction from the work these samples are doing in the research. Each of these studies builds in strategic comparison to its design. The concern in designing these studies is not how many, but what for. The four areas selected in Manchester were identified because they exemplified 'core processes and developing typologies around which individuals could be meaningfully linked' (Savage et al., 2005: 17). The eight areas selected in the US were selected 'to examine suburbs that on the surface would be as different from each other as possible' (Wolfe, 1996: 21), but all exemplified certain characteristics that the researchers considered to be typical of middle class suburbs.

Despite each of these studies using variables and categories to decide where and with whom to sample, neither seeks to make claims that are representative of middle class people of Manchester as a whole, nor the apparently huge self-identified middle class of the United States. As Wolfe (1996: 32) observes:

> despite what, for an ethnographic account, might seem like a relatively high number of interviews, two hundred is far too low a number for any kind of survey.

Instead, in each of these cases the concern is less with knowing what proportion of middle class people thought or acted in this way, and what proportion thought and acted in another way. They are more concerned with capturing complexity, nuance, and the dynamics of the lived experience of being middle class and with exposing and exploring critical cases.

Savage and colleagues' (2005) study is almost unique in tabulating how each of the participants contributed towards the rich narrative account they present in their book, how each individual in their sample supported interpretation and explanation. Arbitrarily choosing one among the 186 participants listed in the appendix, D52, a 39- year-old orchestral musician living in Chorlton, contributes his views on why he decided to move to the area, his love of traditional and changing Manchester, his social and work life, and television viewing habits. Wide ranging views, observations, likes, and feelings are mobilised by Savage and colleagues in the service of their analysis and in the production of cases in the research.

The limits to explanation and the number of cases

Asking an individual about an experience is not to ask them to recount some unique occurrence, but, as Donald T. Campbell (1975) observes, this questioning seeks to provoke a response that allows participants to recount a wealth of experience that relates to the context in which it is described. Participants are chosen because they have this wealth of experience to offer, they have the resource of lived experience to draw on in recounting their story, how these impact on their lives, and the implications of these for social practices. The sample have collected and explained to themselves the collateral experiences of events (March et al., 2003).

As the previous section showed, seeking these accounts from a sample in qualitative research means, inevitably, that from the smallest to the largest qualitative study the sample can only be a fragment. Each of these fragments is a rich elaboration of experiences collected in research. They are not single data points, but detailed stories that elaborate on experience.

In the analytic induction of theoretical or purposive sampling the justification for sample size depends on understanding these experiences in closed social systems. Bertaux and Bertaux-Wiame (1981) (see Table 8.1), for instance, note the relationship between homogeneity of experience and smaller sample sizes and conversely investigations with diverse groups demand a much larger sample. They are conceiving of dissociated critical cases that are brought into conjunction to test the intellectual work in the research. So for instance:

> A single life story stands alone, and it would be hazardous to generalize on the grounds of that one alone, as a second life story could immediately contradict those premature generalizations. But several life stories *taken in the same set of socio-structural relations* support each other and make up, all together, a strong body of evidence (Bertaux and Bertaux-Wiame, 1981: 167 – emphasis in the original).

Bertaux and Bertaux-Wiame are trying to explicate 'the structural patterns that underlie a given set of social processes' (1981: 168). Their typical cases are used to test the vitality of theories about structural relations in the bakery trade (see Chapter 3). An adequate sample is defined by informational redundancy, which is the point when the typical cases are filled with information, but this is a redundancy forever constrained in a given moment in a particular set of contingent and dissociated contextual factors.

For realists, these stories, the accounts of experiences and events (see Chapter 4), do not provide the empirical contours for the production of critical cases. They are, instead, opportunities to test and refine ideas, to prove and refute conjectures. Reporting that 1 or 200 cases were collected is not as important as the ways in which insights into events and experiences are used for interpretation, explanation, and claims from research. Realist sampling strategies seek out extensive accounts that expand upon and develop the descriptive baseline of the chosen cases, providing insight into the ways in which phenomena are experienced, explained, perceived, and accepted in particular contexts and circumstances. Acquiring such insights in research means that what are collected are, invariably, large amounts of data. There are practical challenges to collecting these, which I now consider.

The practical problem of data collection, analysis, and reporting

The detail and richness of narrative we seek in qualitative research mean that it is inevitable that qualitative samples are small. As Mason (2002) notes, there is no methodological reason for small sample sizes in qualitative research, but the sample does have to be of a size that can be managed in practical terms. To return to the study conducted by Savage and colleagues (2005) discussed in the last section, they report collecting nearly 1.5 million words of transcript data. To read all of this data is the equivalent of reading one of Charles Dickens' lengthy novels, Our Mutual Friends for instance, nearly four-and-a-half times over. All of this data need to be transcribed, checked, read, coded, and then parts of these transcripts analysed. It is unsurprising that Savage and colleagues (2005) report that initially they were able to do only data mining to address quite focussed research questions. They finished collecting data in 1999. It was only when Mike Savage had a year of sabbatical from 2002–2003 that the bulk of the data could be analysed. In the meantime the research team took up new jobs, took on administrative responsibilities, no doubt spending much of their time considering how researchers in their respective university departments could do more research, and had to care for their children.

Personal and practical limitations on resources must be at the forefront of researchers' minds when considering how many people's accounts, documents, images, artefacts, places, events, research diary entries or whatever we choose to include in the research.

Qualitative samples are invariably small because in collecting rich insight these data will be bulky. Data can be measured in drawers of filing cabinets filled and hard-drive space consumed. Thrift in planning and implementing a sample must always be tempered, however, with an over-arching concern to ensure enough data is collected to gain insight into the complexity of the social processes under investigation. Parsimony is planned in the research from its early stages of conceptualisation. Frugality and richness of account are constantly accounted for in planning, conducting, and reporting cases in research.

All we have are fragments, experiencing single cases richly

Whether 200 participants or one case is chosen, this choice is made to allow for the interpretation and explaining of social processes. Cases are chosen because they contribute to creatively solving the puzzle under investigation and present as convincing a case as can be mustered with the resources to hand. As noted, Wolfe and Savage are concerned to have enough participants living in each of their predefined areas to say something through comparison about middle class identity, whilst also searching for possible dimensions of difference.

Other researchers may choose quite different tactics. Their concern remains to collect critical cases, and insights that allow for the testing and refining of ideas. It is often reported, for instance, that William Foote Whyte (1993[1943]) chose one slum and one informant in that slum to investigate the highly organised and integrated social system of Cornerville. His informant, Doc, was an entry point into a diverse, but limited network of the slum.

It is experiences in qualitative research like these that Michael Quinn Patton considers in justifying small sample sizes, even the single case study. For Patton (2002: 245) the key considerations in justifying sample size focus around:

> validity, meaningfulness, and insights generated from qualitative inquiry (which) have more to do with the information richness of the cases selected and the observational/analytical capabilities of the researcher than with sample size.

With this observation realists can agree. Patton's pragmatic approach is a two-sided coin. On the one side judgements are made about how to expend resources – an in-depth enquiry with a small number of sources, even a single case. On the other side of the coin are judgements as to whether these pragmatic choices lead to a sufficiently rigorous and valid account of the subject of investigation. Absent, however, from this account are the drivers to evaluate a case's information richness beyond its empirical insight. Realists will be concerned to understand how each case contributes to the work of interpretation and explanation in the research, and how ideas are tested and refined within cases and between cases.

Phillipe Bourgois (1998) shows how a single case is used to work out the relation between ideas and evidence. He pursued his informant Mikey across the wastelands of East Harlem, New York City on a wet and cold December night to learn about taking heroin at the shooting gallery. The striking feature of this study is its thick description; real experiences, recounted and elaborated open up opportunities to work and re-work ideas.

Bourgois (1998: 64–65) seeks to explain the grim reality of the heroin economy. He talks of the

> multi-billion-dollar drug industry – the only growing equal opportunity employer in America's inner cities since the 1970s ... (where) dealers believe with a vengeance in the Great American Dream ... the street offers both a real economic alternative and also an ideological framework that promises pride and self-esteem.

One case brings together observations as Bourgois trailed around after Mikey, learnt from Doc the manager of the shooting gallery, and watched Slim and Flex shoot up speed balls. These empirical accounts are brought into conjunction with theoretical ideas and an account of the context of the study. Together they produce a trustworthy narrative from the research; the grime, cold, fear, desperation, relief, camaraderie, and hierarchy of the shooting gallery are retold. So too are the mechanisms that position agents in a web of structures, convey norms and inter-relationships, interpret and explain causal powers and liabilities. They place Mikey and his fellow addicts in the wastelands of a New York City suburb on a cold winter's night and in a wider canvas of the political economy of the United States. Observation, interview, overheard conversations, accounts of context, and theories are brought to the study, rejected, appropriated, refined, and revised. These are the case in Bourgois' study; a fragment, but one he chooses and uses richly.

Guided by a similarly realist approach Loïc Wacquant opens up life in the Chicago Projects to the interested reader. His sample is Rickey, or more appropriately Rickey's point of view. He is a convenient sample:

> I met Rickey through his brother, whom I had encountered in the course of my research on the craft of the boxer in Chicago in a gym located at the heart of the ghetto ... 'He boxed pro too, he even makin' a comeback, you should interview 'im', suggested Ned. (Wacquant, 1998: 3)

A three hour interview characterised by its 'nervous, up-tempo delivery' (1998: 11) of ghetto living and the life of a hustler gives Wacquant (and most of his readers) an insight into an unknown world, one which Wacquant must position somewhere in time and space:

> Now, it would be a serious mistake to see Rickey as a marginal *curiosa*, an exotic character belonging to a *demi-monde* close to the criminal underworld or liable to an analysis in terms of 'delinquency'. For the hustler, of which he offers a compact personalized incarnation, is on the contrary a *generic figure that occupies a central position* in the social

and symbolic space of the black American ghetto (emphasis in the original).

Wacquant's assertion of the generic space Rickey occupies positions the research in an ethnographic body of slum studies. But the purpose of these is not merely to provide empirical coordinates for his sample. The choice of Latin neuter plural and gender unhinged neologism in this account places him a long way from his subject. Wacquant's job as a social scientist is to bring a deeper understanding of the conditions (Bourdieu, 1996) of Rickey's existence. He draws upon and mobilises theory to explain who his case is and how he will be understood in Wacquant's interpretation of hustling and ghetto life.

We have already learnt that Rickey's narrative cannot be explained through the reductionism of 'delinquency'. Wacquant (1998: 11 – emphasis in the original) places his subject in a wider web of relationships:

> Rickey is not a social anomaly or the representative of a deviant micro-society: rather, he is the *product of the exacerbation of a logic of economic and racial exclusion* that imposes itself ever more stringently on all residents of the ghetto.

In this we have two key features of realist research. First, a rejection of a micro-empirical account in which Rickey is given the tiller-hand. Rickey's interview cannot be read-off as case study, an empiricist representation which attempts, in some way, to convey experience. Even though large parts of the interview are reproduced in the paper, these transcripts do not stand alone. As Bourdieu (1996: 29) argues, '[s]ocial agents do not have an innate knowledge of what they are and what they do [their] declarations can, without aiming to mislead, express quite the opposite of what they appear to say'. Realists must steer these weak constructions with strong interpretation and explanation.

The second key feature highlighted by Wacquant is the engagement of the presuppositions and ideas of the social scientist with evidence; a casing strategy to explain what powers and liabilities work for whom, in what circumstances and why. Wacquant's realist interpretation gives Rickey's tales of the ghetto their theoretical moorings far beyond the boundary of the project. This theory explains the causal mechanisms and the scope of the sample.

If the sample in qualitative research is to do all of this work then it cannot be simply described through the definitiveness and precision of a number. The real world is, as Gian-Carlo Rota (1991: 177) observes, 'filled with absences, with absurdities, with abnormalities, with aberrances, with abominations, with abuses, with *Abgrund* (chasms)'. It is these that are interpreted and explained through our research, which includes the insight of events and experiences from cases, the insiders' perspectives, and the outsiders' understandings.

It is to a brief consideration of this relationship between case and claim that I now turn, before considering the pernicious influence of numbers in descriptions of the sample in qualitative research.

From cases to making claims

Mere empiricism is of little worth, as Boudon (1991) observes. Theories, the claims made from research, are of the middle range. They transcend sheer description or empirical generalisation (Merton, 1968). As seen in the discussion of Wacquant's and Bourgois' realist accounts in the previous section, claims consolidate ideas and evidence into statements that confederate wider networks of theory, yet provide the opportunity to generate hypotheses to be tested through further empirical enquiry. Theories of the middle range are not grand all-encompassing system theories. They are, instead, 'special theories of greater or less scope, coupled with the historically-grounded hope that these will continue to be brought together into families of theories' (Merton, 1968: 48). In other words, theories are fallible, the subject of revision, reinterpretation, and re-presentation. This approach rarely advocates the wholesale ditching of an idea, but is one of constant accretion (Pawson, 2013).

All research, as I argued in Chapter 4, starts with ideas. The problems chosen for research do not come out of the blue but are related to our background knowledge. Investigations are driven by ideas, the sample is chosen using these ideas. From this sample we gain descriptive narratives of events and experiences. This sample may be animate units able to express events and experiences, such as individuals, groups, or organisations. Similarly, our sample may comprise inanimate traces of the relations between structure and agency in documents, photographs, or even the contents of a family's mantelpiece.

Howsoever the sample is composed of sampling units they provide empirical subjective insight. These narratives are, as Margaret Archer (2000: 313) observes, 'about the world and therefore cannot be independent from the way the world is'. For realists there is no direct correspondence between that which we observe, hear, or see, and reality. Social reality cannot be simply captured in description or, for that matter, ideas. It is far richer and deeper than that. Provisional theories about reality are tested, refined, and judged in relation to evidence. This evidence must support conclusions and conclusions must not go beyond what the evidence can support, as Howard Becker (in Baker and Edwards, 2012: 15) argues.

These data may be from samples of one or fewer, as James G. March and colleagues (2003: 469) have it. They 'provide scraps of information about an underlying reality that cumulate, much the way various elements of a portrait cumulate to provide information about its subject'. They are fragments. These are neither independent samples of some universe in a statistical sense, nor will they cumulate to signify a wider population.

In a realist sampling strategy, purposive work allows for a plan to be drawn up of the number of units to be sampled early in the research. These numbers are a plan only, in which ideas, external and internal powers in the research provide an account of the number of observations to be carried out, the interviews conducted, the documents read, and so on. This quota will inevitably change as the research progresses and insight is gained into that which is investigated. As discussed in Chapter 6, the variables used to define quotas presented in early plans are less a blueprint and more a preliminary sketch on the back of an envelope. They are there to be elaborated on as the research progresses.

In common with the inductive strategy, cases in a realist strategy are, as was noted in the previous chapter, subject to processes of repeated and reflexive planning in the research. In answering the question 'how many qualitative interviews is enough?' (Baker and Edwards, 2012: 29) Jennifer Mason's response in this working paper is, 'it depends'. The web of considerations upon which the judgement is made is these:

a deep exploration of how processes work in particular contexts, under certain sets of circumstances, and in particular sets of social relations ... a more interpretative and investigative logic ... so that you build a convincing analytical narrative based on the argument that you have explored the process in its richness, complexity and detail, and that you have understood the contingency of different contexts.

What Mason argues for here is strongly interpretative. The quota of contexts, circumstances, and social relations will start with a number for practical reasons. Cases will be described and re-described throughout the research. Ideas are brought into play with evidence through its collection and interpretation. Cases bear these characteristics as the relation between ideas and evidence are worked out through the research.

Yet frequently the breaks are put on this reflexive process and the sample is quantified. It is asserted that a particular size of sample is adequate to investigate a research question. Often this insistence on a larger sample size is imposed by external liabilities and powers: ethics review boards, journal reviewers (an example of which I discuss shortly), grant proposal reviewers, examiners, and academic supervisors who are worried by all of the above. A pseudo-quantitative logic is imposed that assumes a large number sample is more reliable towards producing trustworthy findings from research.

Pronouncements from external powers to increase sample size can be explained through the imposition of a dominant ideology of quantitative reasoning. Yet, it is surprising, even intriguing, how many qualitative methodologists advocate an acceptable sample size for qualitative studies. It is to this allure of numbers that I now turn.

The allure of the number n

There are no guidelines, tests of adequacy, or power calculations available to establish sample size in qualitative research. Yet qualitative researchers persist in using a mathematical notation (n) to describe their sample size. This is emphasised in Table 8.1 which reports how qualitative researchers have found it necessary to state that particular kinds of studies across qualitative idioms require a particular sample size or range. In most of these examples no evidence is provided for the chosen range. The impression gained from reading the accounts in which these assertions are made is that this sample size worked in a specific study undertaken to investigate a particular phenomenon, with a particular population, in a particular setting (see for instance Morse (1994) and Creswell (1998) in Table 8.1). Given that replicating studies to account for these dimensions is highly unlikely, generalising from these numbers and applying them is not productive to the research of others. The guidance offered in Table 8.1 has little if any value in determining sample size in qualitative studies.

Table 8.1   The limited value of stating n in qualitative research studies

Author	Sample size (n)	Notes
Bertaux and Bertaux-Wiame (1981)	15–30	Depends on the variety of structural experience – based on research with bakers (homogeneous group) bakery owners (heterogeneous group)
Kuzel (1992)	6–8	Homogeneous sample (assertion, no evidence)
	12–20	Heterogeneous sample – 'when looking for disconfirming evidence or trying to achieve maximum variation' (assertion, no evidence)
Morse (1994)	6	Phenomenological studies (assertion, no evidence)
	35	Ethnographies, grounded theory studies, ethnoscience (assertion, no evidence)
	100–200	Qualitative ethology (detailed study of behaviour) (assertion, no evidence)
Creswell (1998)	5–25	Phenomenological studies (assertion, no evidence)
	20–30	Grounded theory studies (assertion, no evidence)

Author	Sample size (n)	Notes
Bernard (2000)	36	Most ethnographic studies seem to be based on this number (assertion, no evidence)
Guest et al. (2006: 79)	12	'For most research enterprises ... in which the aim is to understand common perceptions and experiences among a group of relatively homogeneous individuals, twelve interviews should suffice.'
Adler and Adler in Baker and Edwards (2012)	30	A good round number to aim for (a practical consideration and acceptable to external powers)
	12	A student's one semester study (a practical opportunity to practice qualitative research skills)
	20	A student's two semester study (a practical opportunity to practice qualitative research skills)

The limits of theoretical saturation

The most commonly mentioned justification for a stated sample size in qualitative research, Mark Mason (2010) assures us, is theoretical saturation. This is based on his extensive review of PhD studies using qualitative methods. Theoretical saturation is described across the approaches to grounded theory discussed in Chapter 1. Corbin and Strauss (2008) suggest that less than 5–6 interviews are not enough to achieve saturation but do not identify quite how large a sample should be. Mason (2010) in his investigation of 560 PhD studies found that a mean average sample size of 31, but with a widespread distribution (standard deviation 18.7). There was, Mark Mason went on to note, a preponderance of studies including 10, 20, 30, and 40 participants.

It is intriguing to ask why the mean average is 31. One reason may be that 30 degrees of freedom is when Student's t-distribution used for small n samples in statistics approximates to a normal distribution, an unwritten pseudo-quantitative logic that 30 is a small sample in statistical research so it will do for qualitative research with its small sample sizes. Of course this is just lateral thinking, but of more concern in a discussion about sample size is Mason's observation that PhD students are not adhering to guidelines for theoretical saturation. He contends that the problem with these guidelines is their elasticity. Yet, Greg Guest, Arwan Bunce, and Laura Johnson (2006) felt able to devise a sophisticated experiment to quantify when theoretical saturation is achieved suggesting that these guidelines can be rigorously applied.

147

The definition of theoretical saturation Guest and colleagues (2006: 65) use is 'the point in data collection and analysis when new information produces little or no change to the codebook'. Their experiment is designed to gain a 'reliable sense of thematic exhaustion and variability within … the data set'.

This experiment asks several key questions of theoretical saturation. How many interviews are needed before no new codes are discovered? How many interviews are needed before codes are filled and no further empirical data is needed? And finally, what value is there to the study through using comparative groups? The experiment addresses the key dimensions of theoretical saturation as discussed by Glaser and Strauss (1967) and which Glaser (2001: 191) summarises:

> Saturation is not seeing the same pattern over and over again. It is the conceptualisation of comparisons of these incidents which yield different properties of the pattern, until no new properties of the pattern emerge. This yields the conceptual density that when integrated into hypotheses make up the body of the generated grounded theory with theoretical completeness.

Guest and colleagues conduct their experiment within a study to investigate the accuracy with which women who fall into a high risk group of acquiring HIV infection talk about their sexual encounters. Thirty sex workers were recruited in Ibaban, Nigeria and Accra, Ghana, from three high-risk sites, a red light area, a hotel, and a hostel. The criteria for selection were that the women were eighteen years of age or older; had vaginal sex with more than one male partner in the previous three months; and had vaginal sex three or more times in an average week. Each woman was asked identical questions in the same order from an interview guide, but the interviewers were encouraged to ask a number of sub-questions if particular issues were raised. Interviewers were also encouraged to probe key themes.

Working with batches of six transcripts (the smallest recommended sample size these authors identified in the literature), Guest and colleagues audited the newly created codes and changes to existing code definitions. They measured the frequency with which codes were applied. Starting with the interviews collected in Ghana, these sedulous researchers coded the interviews six at a time until all 30 were coded, then moved on to add the analysis of the codes collected from Nigeria until all 60 interviews had been audited.

The final codebook was made up of 109 content-driven codes, of which 80 (73%) were identified in the first six interviews. A further 20 (18%) were identified in the next six. After analysis of the first 12 interviews, 92% of the codes had been discovered. After reviewing all thirty interviews from Ghana the researchers completed their codebook. They moved on to the Nigerian data, adding one more substantive code and developing four of the codes as variations on existing codes. 'Two of the four new codes were needed for the unique sub-group of campus-based sex workers' (Guest et al., 2006: 66). This group neither referred to themselves as sex workers, nor to their sexual partners as clients. The codes were modified to account for the different ways in which this sub-group talked about themselves and clients.

The first part of this audit revealed the frequency of coding. The second investigated how codes changed as the research progressed. In all, 36 changes were made to codes during the research; eleven percent in the first round of analysis, the largest number of change in the second round (17 changes, 47%), and 20 percent of changes in the third round. By the time 18 interviews had been audited, 78% of the changes had been made to codes.

A third test sought to identify the thematic importance of each code, through identifying the internal consistency of participants' accounts. After the first 18 interviews, participants were consistently addressing all the most important themes identified in the research. The most frequently discussed themes were elaborated on in the early interviews. Thirty-six codes were mentioned frequently by participants, of these 34 (94%) were mentioned in the first six interviews, and 35 (97%) after 12 interviews. Guest and colleagues conclude that very little was missed in the early stages of analysis.

This experiment investigates two of the three themes Glaser and Strauss (1967) consider with reference to theoretical saturation, the empirical limits of the data in producing codes, and the depth of each category. Their experiment meets Glaser's demand that theoretical saturation should include approaches to coding and refining of these codes to aid conceptual density. But Guest and colleagues (2006) did not seek to develop different slices of data through using different research instruments, the third element of Glaser and Strauss's schema for theoretical saturation. The semi-structured interview instrument applied by Guest and colleagues was, in fact, quite rigid and was applied with all 60 of their participants. This has important implications for any interpretation of the results from this experiment and its application to other studies.

The important finding from this research is that after 12 interviews 100 of the 107 codes (93.45%) are discovered and 97% of the changes are made to these codes. In an objectivist grounded theory logic of theoretical saturation a very large proportion of empirical findings have emerged, and, therefore, theory discovered. Guest and colleagues (2006) question whether there is much value in doing more than 12 interviews. The final 38 interviews produce only marginal returns of theory discovery for a large expenditure of resources.

At first sight, mobilising a comparison does not seem particularly fruitful towards identifying new codes or saturating existing codes either. This experiment does not report on differences between the three high-risk sites used to access participants in each country. The emergence of new codes and the refining of codes were very small when the Nigerian data were added to and compared with the Ghanaian data. Part of the explanation may rest in the similarity of experience between sex workers in the two countries, although Guest and colleagues (2006) do highlight apparently important differences between the two country groups. This lack of discovery is intriguing and does raise questions as to why further insights that produced new codes and refined existing codes did not happen. Part of the answer may lie in the openness and theoretical sensitivity of the researchers in each country. As Guest and colleagues (2005) observe in another paper, there was an important methodological difference between the interviews conducted in Ghana and Nigeria. Despite the interviewers in both countries using the same semi-structured interview instrument and receiving the same training, the 'Nigerian interviewers did not probe responses as readily, rendering significantly shorter responses' (2005: 287).

$n = 12$, how reassuring?

Guest and colleagues' paper, *How many interviews are enough? An experiment with data saturation and variability* (2006) has become reassuringly useful to some qualitative researchers seeking a justification for sample size. I have heard at least one PhD supervisor observe that she tells her students their sample size should be $n=12$, based on this paper. A recent blog in Methodspace makes a similar argument, referring to one of the external powers discussed above:

> I and a recent doc. student grad. have had difficulty with some journal review boards with the small sample size of qualitative research. I have tried to communicate the point that saturation is more important than the sample size. Does anyone have any references that may discuss sample size in qualitative research? …

> My student had 4 participants, 2 rounds of interviews and member checks with each for a total of 12 interviews. Guest, Bunce, and Johnson (2006) found with their study that involved 60 interviews theme saturation was achieved after 12 interviews. I use[d] their study as [it] supported my student's decision.

> <http://www.methodspace.com/forum/topics/sample-size-and-number-of?id=2289984%3ATopic%3A12428&page=1#comments>

Guest and colleagues (2006) emphasise considerable care should be exercised when relying on the authority of their experiment to justify theoretical saturation and sample size. First they note that such small samples might well work if those with whom research is being done share common experiences. Many of the women in their study experienced fear of being exposed as sex workers by the media, and according to the authors they work in very similar contexts. The samples' experiences are relatively homogeneous. The study design reinforces this homogeneity through its fairly limited research questions. It enquired into a narrow range of experiences, with, as discussed above, each participant asked a similar set of questions. Guest and colleagues (2006) consider that without these factors – a relatively homogeneous substantive experience that is widespread in the target population, and a narrowly-focussed and prescribed method – the ability to achieve theoretical saturation in a grounded theory methodology cannot be reached. Their finding, that $n=12$ interviews is sufficient, is 'not applicable to unstructured and highly exploratory interview techniques', where saturation 'would be a moving target, as new responses are given to newly introduced questions.' (2006: 75).

As soon as the phenomenon under investigation is recognised to be dynamic, contingent, and best explored through detailed and in-depth investigation, then the principles of theoretical saturation demonstrate considerable weaknesses.

There is also compelling evidence of a feedback mechanism at play between a narrowness of approach and a narrowness of theoretical discovery through coding in this experiment. The lack of new codes emerging from the very different sex workers in Nigeria is surprising. Part of this might arise from the lack of training among the Nigerian researchers, as noted. But a further element could well be what Dey (2007) describes as theoretical sufficiency, in which categories suggested by data rely on researchers' conjecture. They stop short of coding all data through applying a strictly enforced search for themes and codes, which in turn foreclose possibilities for innovative and creative interpretation and explanation from the events and experiences being coded. The emphasis is on coding as simplifying or reducing complexity rather than complicating data through its conceptualisation, 'raising questions, and providing provisional answers about the relations among and within the data', as Amanda Coffey and Paul Atkinson (1996: 31) suggest should happen in any process of data analysis.

Guest and colleagues (2006) take the simplifying approach to coding. The numbers game, how many interviews, observations, focus groups, documents, units, or whatever are enough, rests on an empiricist and positivist assumption that the insight from qualitative research is the sum of the parts, appropriately collected, reduced, and processed to provide descriptive answers.

Charmaz (2006), who, as argued in Chapter 1, seeks to distance her account of a constructivist grounded theory from its positivist roots, contends that objectivist methodologies of grounded theory have the potential to 'force data into preconceived frameworks ... (it) takes the focusing inherent in grounded theory and renders it directive and prescriptive' (2006: 115). As she also observes, Guest and colleagues' result of 12 interviews 'may generate themes, but not respect' (Charmaz in Baker and Edwards, 2012: 21).

Respect, she argues, comes from recognising the wealth of insight that should come from mixed qualitative research methods. Beyond these observations Charmaz does not distance herself from the micro-empiricism of grounded theory, however. Her solution to the foreclosure of interpretation inherent in objectivist grounded theory is to return to the data, to recode it towards defining new leads. Researchers should, in Henwood and Pidgeon's terms:

> avoid being wedded to particular theoretical positions and key studies in the literature in ways that overtly direct ways of looking and stymies the interactive process of engagement with the empirical world studied. Theoretical agnosticism is a better watchword than theoretical ignorance ... (2003: emphasis in the original).

Theory falls out of the data in this account of its co-construction. It is a re-framing of Glaser and Strauss's insistence on openness and theoretical sensitivity, underwritten by an assumption that it is the number of engagements with the empirical world that are key, even if the emphasis is on depth of engagement as well as breadth. Saturation, whether configured through an objectivist or constructivist approach to grounded theory insists that size of the sample matters. Both approaches assume that theoretical saturation arises from the neutrality of the researcher in their coding of data, and from this coding we can determine a number, a count of data points where as Morse (1995: 148) observes in the objectivist tradition, there is 'enough data to build a comprehensive and convincing theory', and Charmaz (2006: 114) contends, from a constructivist standpoint that 'a study of 25 interviews may suffice for certain small projects but invites scepticism when the author's claims are about, say, human nature or contradict established research'.

Making the sample work

In 1659, Blaise Pascal observed that 'nature confutes the sceptics, reason confutes the dogmatists' (translated and quoted in Lakatos, 1976: 54). Put more plainly, realists will always find their explanation of nature wanting, empiricists will find their methods inadequate for the task.

Drawing on more recent debates, the empiricism of grounded theory and theoretical sampling was the focus of Chapter 1. Grounded theory hinges on concerns that the procedures to transform empirical data points to theory through coding are correct. Theoretical saturation, similarly, appears to offer a method through which claims can be made for the adequacy of a sample size in a study. As I have shown, however, such claims to saturation can only be made through simplifying and reducing the complexity of insight.

The selection of information rich cases is the preferred strategy of purposeful or judgemental sampling strategies. These empirical cases can be evaluated for their rigour. They are sufficient for the enquiry of which they are part. The number of cases is part of this pragmatic consideration too. Sample size is evaluated in a similar way to the choice of which of the 14+1 strategies of purposeful sampling should be applied in a particular study (see Chapter 2), which strategy most adequately reflects observed reality in the most convincing way for its intended audience.

The strong interpretation of inductive strategies of theoretical or purposive sampling takes the discussion about sample size in yet another direction. The critical case combines intellectual work with the empirical contours in the research. As was discussed in Chapter 3, the task is to build explanation of how social processes work in particular contexts, within certain social relations, and under particular circumstances. This deep exploration interprets the conditions under which causal relations operate, through strategic comparison of cases, whether considered typical or negative. The case is achieved through its closure, dissociating it from anything other than the causal powers that are being investigated. In this way sample size is always justified in relation to the explanation from the research. There is sufficient information to interpret the 'experience' as a 'complex interactional process involving many happenings and events' (Lindesmith, 1968: 13 – emphasis in the original), any more insight would be redundant. Induction is found wanting in its explanation of nature. Nature is an open system. For realists, samples are always fragments drawn from this open and stratified system.

The focus of any realist justification of the cases chosen in the research is on the adequacy (O'Reilly and Parker, 2012) of the data collected. These justifications are constantly informed by preconceived theory that shapes the choices we make about whom or what to sample. The task is to demonstrate how the fragments available are used towards explanation and interpretation. The consideration in a realist sampling strategy is what work we can set the sample to do in the research to test, refine, and adjudicate between ideas.

There is no reasonable methodological way in which realist qualitative researchers can tell you the eventual number of cases in advance. If they provide a number it is likely that they are complying with external liabilities and powers from institutions, ethics review boards, funding bodies, and/or editors of journals. They are obliged to assume that those who review their research are beguiled by a pseudo-quantitative logic. They hold that a largish number (generally ≥ 30) of interviews, focus groups, or whatever instruments chosen, equates with a trustworthy outcome from the study.

Quite often a number is stated in research plans and proposals. This can be interpreted as a sample size. It is not. This number is an estimate, based on evaluation of human and financial resources available. It will include a calculation of the number of times research instruments are used and an estimate of the time to recruit participants, apply the instrument, and deal with the data generated, use these in interpretative and explanatory work in the research, and disseminate the knowledge generated. In addition, any count of potential units to be sampled will include purposive work, the incomplete accounts of who or what would be useful to do research with, a given number of units that have a given set of characteristics chosen towards testing and refining theories of the middle range.

While this work is often done, the sample size stated at the beginning of the study will not be reflected in the final account of the cases. This casing is done for two reasons. First, the descriptive baseline of units chosen to be studied is continuously extended throughout the research. That which we thought we sampled initially is not what we realise we cased eventually. Secondly, we will work and rework the relationships between ideas and fragmentary evidence throughout the research. This is the methodological work of casing. A number can be assigned, eventually, to the number of cases in any piece of research, but it is not the number of cases that matters, it is what you do with them that counts. Sample size are frequently used to determine the quality of both qualitative and quantitative research design, as Emma Uprrichard (2013b: 7) observes. But in realist research this criteria is rendered meaningless 'without further explanation as to what, how and why [it] may matter in the first place.'

In the introduction to this book I suggested choosing cases in qualitative research is better understood through inverting the traditional account of sampling. In realist qualitative research the sample can only be weakly elaborated beforehand. It is at best a weak construction which raises consciousness about the cases in the research and why they are chosen. Little of value can be said about what these will represent at the outset, but a great deal will be learnt as the research progresses. Descriptions will change from fragile accounts using variables and categories to strong interpretations and explanations incorporating causal mechanisms, contexts and outcomes.

There is no methodological reason for ensuring that every person or thing from a predefined population has the same chance of inclusion in an investigation. A strategy for choosing cases that is random or stratified may be designed into the study for particular theoretical reasons. But, like strategies, cases are chosen because they can be worked and reworked through the research. Choosing cases provides opportunities to interpret and explain social phenomena, and the powers of these things that exist independent of our accounts of them, as best we can.

9

CHOOSING CASES IN
QUALITATIVE RESEARCH

I conclude through identifying the key methodological and practical features of choosing cases in qualitative research in a realist approach.

In a realist sampling strategy, as is common across all the strategies discussed in this book, it is not appropriate to lift definitions of sampling from quantitative research and apply their logic to qualitative research. The acts of defining a population through using variables to describe observable characteristics and ensuring that every individual unit in that pre-defined population has an equal and measurable chance of inclusion in research cannot be applied.

Even so, sampling and sample are commonly used terms across methods of qualitative research. I have argued the verb sampling does not do justice to the acts of choosing cases in a realist approach. Similarly, the noun sample, with its emphasis on a unit drawn from a pre-defined population, fails to get at the ways in which cases are chosen. The purpose of qualitative research is to interpret and explain the complex things that sustain cases. Choosing cases is a far better way to describe the way in which scientific realist qualitative research proceeds.

Realism

The realism discussed in this book is a model of a stratified reality being composed generatively. By which I mean social reality is not simply captured by descriptions of events and experiences, it is far richer and deeper than these empirical features of the social, practical, and natural world. The second feature of this model is that it is an open social system.

These two key features set a realist strategy of choosing cases apart from the three strategies of sampling discussed in the first part of the book:

- The versions of theoretical sampling discussed in Chapter 1 are arrayed along a continuum from objectivist (positivist) to constructivist grounded theory. They are connected by a common theme of empiricism, which for realists is of little worth.

- The pragmatic strategy of purposeful sampling discussed in Chapter 2 is similarly empiricist in its search for information rich cases and an appropriate rendering of these cases. What is emphasised in this account of 14+1 strategies for sampling is the importance of researchers using their judgement in choosing strategies and combinations of strategies to best research a particular social phenomenon. This is an important insight to a realist sampling strategy, but it is ideas not data that guide choices.
- The intellectual work of researchers is central to the theoretical or purposive sampling strategy, the focus of Chapter 3. With this working out of the relation between theory and empirical contours in research realists can agree. Where a realist approach parts company from this strongly inductive approach is in the assumption that this intellectual work will lead to the closure of the case and claims that the case under investigation is typical; it is representative of a population identified through research practice. For realists the descriptive baseline is forever extending.

In realist research, cases can never be typical because they are composed generatively. These generative mechanisms have the power to affect behaviour and make a difference. They have causal efficacy which establishes the reality of social objects. It is these powers, liabilities, and dispositions that are interpreted and explained in both the social phenomena under investigation and the cases chosen to investigate these in research.

Realist research seeks to work out the relation between ideas and evidence, between insiders' perspectives and experiences of events, and outsiders understandings of the causal mechanisms that bring about change. Interpretations and explanations are always provisional. They are expressed as models to be transferred from one complex system to another to be tested, refined, and elaborated. These models seek to explain what works for whom in what circumstances and why. All research must bracket its claims, and realist research is no different. Cases are ecologically bounded to produce an identity, an expression of connections and context in a complex open system.

In Part Two of this book, I sought to address these challenges and proposed a model of choosing cases in qualitative research comprising purposive work, the purposeful selection of cases, and the working and re-working of these cases as casing to meet these challenges of interpretation and explanation.

Purposive work

In a realist strategy of choosing cases, theory (or put less grandly, ideas), always precedes the collection of evidence. Researchers bring prejudices, pre-judgements, theories, frames of reference, and concepts to their choices. These concepts, meanings, and intentions are as real as the table I am sitting at writing, just not as accessible to direct observation and description.

Alongside these concepts, which are best described as the internal powers in the choosing of cases, are external powers. There are structures, like the institutions we work for and who fund research and the participants with whom we conduct research, which motivate, constrain, discourage, and enable certain sorts of research. They interpose in the choices of cases.

Purposive work sets the scene for a programme of revision, elaboration, and reconstruction of theory. In a realist strategy of choosing cases there is no convenience sample, purposeful choices are always bootstrapped by presuppositions as ideas.

The purposeful choices of cases

In the reflexive and interpretative engagement of purposive work, embryonic theories are constructed and propositional statements elaborated, which are nonetheless bold. Cases are chosen to build systems to test, refine, and elaborate theories of the middle range (which are a set of statements that organise ideas and relate them to evidence). New cases become strategic when they challenge and re-specify received causal processes.

Cases are composed generatively to test and extend theories of the middle range. Realism thrives on counter-instances, events and experiences that are anomalies to be explained and integrated into a theory.

As important as strategically choosing cases is recognising that cases are transformed in research. When cases are first chosen they are invariably described using variables, which refer to traces of real systems. But the descriptions of cases will change throughout the research as the relation between ideas and evidence is worked out. These are methodological acts of casing in the research.

Casing

Casing is used to build systems through which sets of ideas can be judged against evidence, which is situation specific wisdom of events and experiences. The question 'what is this a case of?' is asked repeatedly throughout the research and is never fully answered. This strategy of casing transforms the cases in the research through configuring, reconfiguring, fusing, and splitting cases to best resolve relationships between ideas and evidence, a system built to compare, juxtapose, and judge ideas.

This transformation means that the description of units, purposefully chosen in the early research, will be considerably extended in the final account of cases. This is the same as saying, that which we thought we sampled initially is not what we realise we cased eventually. Casing, as working out the relation between ideas and evidence, undermines a pseudo-quantitative pre-occupation with the size of the sample. A realist account of choosing cases recognises that a number can be assigned, eventually, to the number of cases in any piece of research. But, it is not the number of cases that matters, it is the work they are shown to do in interpretation and explanation that counts.

Conclusion

The cases chosen and worked and reworked throughout the research allow for an explanation of the zigzag route of investigation, which is the sifting, winnowing, and refining of ideas.

In the introduction to this book I suggested choosing cases in qualitative research is better understood through inverting the traditional description of sampling. In realist qualitative research the sample can only be weakly elaborated beforehand. It is at best a weak construction which raises consciousness about the cases in the research and why they are chosen. A great deal will be learnt about these cases as the research progresses. Descriptions will change from fragile embryonic accounts using variables and categories to strong interpretations and explanations incorporating causal mechanisms, contexts and outcomes to explain what works for whom in what circumstance and why, when and so on, in the complexity of the social world.

In considering these complexities and the implication for choosing cases in qualitative research, I am reminded of the cases Walter Benjamin collected, in his Arcades Project in Paris, with their incompleteness, additions, revisions, formulations, reformulations, and retrievals (Benjamin, 1999). When Hannah Arendt (1971: 51) discusses Benjamin's method more broadly she invokes Ariel's song from *The Tempest*, and in doing so captures the essence of the work a researcher choosing cases must do in qualitative research:

> Like a pearl diver who descends to the bottom of the sea, not to excavate the bottom and bring it to light but to pry loose … the pearls and corals in the depths, … as 'thought fragments', as something 'rich and strange', and perhaps even a (relatively enduring) phenomenon.

REFERENCES

Abbott, A. (2001) *Chaos and disciplines*. Chicago: University of Chicago Press.

American Anthropological Association (1998) 'Code of ethics of the American Anthropological Association', < http://www.aaanet.org/issues/policy-advocacy/Code-of-Ethics.cfm > accessed May 2013.

Archer, M. (1998) 'Realism and morphogenesis', in M. Archer et al. (eds), *Critical realism: essential readings*. London: Routledge, pp. 356–382.

Archer, M. (2000) *Being human: the problem of agency*. Cambridge: Cambridge University Press.

Arendt, H. (1971) 'Walter Benjamin: 1892–1940', in W. Benjamin (ed.), *Illuminations*. London: Fontana/Collins.

Baker, S. E. and Edwards, R. (2012) *How many qualitative interviews is enough?* NCRM, National Centre for Research Methods Review Paper.

Benjamin, W. (1999) *The Arcades Project*. Cambridge Massachusetts: Harvard University Press.

Bernard, H. R. (2000) *Social research methods*. Thousand Oaks, CA: SAGE.

Bertaux, D. and Bertaux-Wiame, I. (1981) 'Life stories in the Bakers' trade', in D. Bertaux (ed.), *Biography and society: the life history approach in the social sciences*. London: SAGE, pp. 169–190.

Bhaskar, R. (1979) *The possibility of naturalism: a philosophical critique of the contemporary human sciences*. London: Routledge.

Bhaskar, R. (2008) *A realist theory of science*. London: Verso.

Blaikie, N. (2010) *Designing social research*. Bristol: Polity Press.

Blumer, H. (1956) 'Sociological analysis and the "variable"', *American Sociological Review*, vol. 21, no. 6, pp. 683–660.

Blumer, H. (1978) 'Methodological principles of empirical science', in N. K. Denzin (ed.), *Sociological methods: a sourcebook*. New York: McGraw Hill.

Bobadilla, J. L., Frenk, J., Lozano, R., Frejka, T. and Stern, C. (1993) 'The epidemiological transition and health priorities', in D. T. Jamison et al. (eds), *Disease control priorities in developing countries*. Bombay: Oxford Medical Publications for the World Bank.

Boudon, R. (1991) 'What middle-range theories are', *Contemporary Sociology*, vol. 20, pp. 519–522.

Bourdieu, P. (1996) 'Understanding', *Theory, Culture & Society*, vol. 13, no. 2, pp. 17–37.

Bourdieu, P. (2002) *The weight of the world: social suffering in contemporary society*. Cambridge: Polity Press.

Bourgois, P. (1998) 'Just another night in a shooting gallery', *Theory, Culture and Society*, vol. 15, no. 2, pp. 37–66.

Bowley, A. L. (1906) 'Address to the Economic Science and Statistics Section of the British Association for the Advancement of Science', *Journal of the Royal Statistical Society*, vol. 69, pp. 540–558.

Brody, H., Rip, M. R., Vinten-Johansen, P., Paneth, N. and Rachman, S. (2000) 'Map-making and myth-making in Broad Street: the London cholera epidemic, 1854', *Lancet*, vol. 35661, pp. 64–68.

Browne, A. (1987) *When battered women kill*. London: Collier Macmillan.

Browne, K. (2005) 'Snowball sampling: using social networks to research non-heterosexual women', *International Journal of Social Research Methodology*, vol. 8, no. 1, pp. 47–60.

Bryant, A. (2003) 'A constructive/ist response to Glaser', *Forum Qualitative Sozialforschung/Forum: Qualitative Social Research; Vol 3, No 3 (2002): Subjectivity and Reflexivity in Qualitative Research I*, vol. 4, no. 1.

Burawoy, M. (2009) *The extended case method and one theoretical tradition*. Los Angeles: University of California Press.

Byrne, D. (2002) *Interpreting quantitative data*. London: SAGE.

Byrne, D. (2012) 'UK sociology and quantitative methods: are we as weak as they think? Or are they barking up the wrong tree?', *Sociology*, vol. 46, no. 1, pp. 13–24.

Campbell, D. T. (1975) '"Degrees of Freedom" and the case study', *Comparative Political Studies*, vol. 8, no. 2, pp. 178–193.

Carter, B. and New, C. (2004) 'Realist social theory and empirical research', in B. Carter and C. New (eds), *Making realism work: realist social theory and empirical research*. London: Routledge.

Charmaz, K. (2000) 'Grounded theory: objectivist and constructivist methods', in N. K. Denzin and Y. S. Lincoln (eds), *Handbook of qualitative research, Second Edition*. Thousand Oaks, CA: SAGE.

Charmaz, K. (2006) *Constructing grounded theory*. London: SAGE.

Charmaz, K. (2009) 'Shifting the grounds: constructivist grounded theory methods', in J. Morse et al. (eds), *Developing grounded theory: the second generation*. Walnut Creek CA: Left Coast Press.

Clark, A. (2007) 'Understanding communities: a review of networks, ties, and contacts', *NCRM Working Paper. ESRC National Centre for Research Methods*.

Clark, T. (2008) '"We're Over-Researched Here!"', *Sociology*, vol. 42, no. 5, pp. 953–970.

Clarke, A. E. (2009) 'From grounded theory to situational analysis', in J. Morse et al. (eds), *Developing grounded theory: the second generation*. Walnut Creek CA: Left Coast Press.

Coffey, A. and Atkinson, P. (1996) *Making sense of qualitative data: complementary research strategies*. London: SAGE.

Corbin, J. and Strauss, A. (2008) *Basics of qualitative research: techniques and procedures for developing grounded theory*. London: SAGE.

Creswell, J. (1998) *Qualitative inquiry and research design: choosing among five traditions*. Thousand Oaks, CA: SAGE.

Danermark, B., Ekström, M., Jakobsen, L. and Karlsson, J. C. (1997) *Explaining society: critical realism in the social sciences*. London: Routledge.

Daston, L. and Galison, P. (2007) *Objectivity*. New York: Zone Books.

Davies, K. (2011) 'Knocking on doors: recruitment and enrichment in a qualitative interview-based study', *International Journal of Social Research Methodology*, vol. 14, no. 4, pp. 289–300.

Deutsch, D. (2011) *The beginning of infinity: explanations that transform the world*. Harmondsworth: Penguin Press.

Dey, I. (2007) *Grounding grounded theory: guidelines for qualitative inquiry*. Bingley: JAI Press.

Edwards, R., Ribbens, J. and Gillies, V. (1999) 'Shifting boundaries and power in the research process: the example of researching "step families"', in J. Seymour and P. Bagguley (eds), *Relating intimacies*. New York: St Martin's Press.

Elliott, J. (1999) 'Models are stories are not real life', in D. Dorling and S. Simpson (eds), *Statistics in society*. London: Arnold.

Elliott, J., Miles, A., Parsons, S. and Savage, M. (2010) 'The design and content of the "Social Participation" study: a qualitative sub-study conducted as part of the age 50 (2008) sweep of the National Child Development Study', *CLS Cohort Studies Working Paper*. Center of Longitudinal Studies. Institute of Education, University of London.

Emirbayer, M. and Mische, A. (1998) 'What is agency?', *American Journal of Sociology*, vol. 103, no. 4, pp. 962–1023.

Emmel, N. D. (1998) *Perceptions of health and the value placed on health care deliverers in the slums of Bombay*. Leeds: The University of Leeds, PhD Thesis (unpublished).

Emmel, N. D. and Clark, A. (2009) *The methods used in Connected Lives*. ESRC National Center for Research Methods, <eprints.ncrm.ac.uk/.../2009_connected_lives_methods_emmel_clark>.

Emmel, N. D. and Hughes, K. (2009) 'Small-N access cases to refine theories of social exclusion and access to socially excluded individuals and groups', in D. Byrne and C. Ragin (eds), *The Sage Handbook of Case-Based Methods*. London: SAGE.

Emmel, N. D., Hughes, K., Greenhalgh, J. and Sales, A. (2007) 'Accessing socially excluded people. Trust and the gatekeeper in the researcher–participant relationship', *Sociological Research Online*, vol. 12, no. 2:

Finch, J. and Mason, J. (1990) 'Decision taking in the fieldwork process: theoretical sampling and collaborative working', in R. G. Burgess (ed.) *Studies in Qualitative Methodology Volume 2*, JAI Press. Bingley, pp. 25–50.

French, S. and Ladyman, J. (2003) 'Remodeling structural realism: quantum physics and the metaphysics of structure', *Synthese*, vol. 136, pp. 31–56.

Gallup, G. (1944) *A guide to public opinion polls*. Princeton: Princeton University Press.

Gardiner, J., Stuart, M., MacKenzie, R., Forde, C., Greenwood, I. and Perrett, R. (2009) 'Redundancy as a critical life event: moving on from the Welsh steel industry through career change', *Work, employment and society*, vol. 23, no. 4, pp. 727–745.

Geertz, C. (1973) *The interpretation of cultures: selected essays*. Basic: New York.

Geertz, C. (1988) *Works and lives: the anthropologist as author*. Cambridge: Polity.

Glaser, B. (1978) *Theoretical sensitivity*. Mill Hill CA: The Sociology Press.

Glaser, B. (2001) *The grounded theory perspective: conceptualization contrasted with description*. Mill Hill CA: The Sociology Press.

Glaser, B. G. (1992) *Basics of grounded theory analysis: emergence vs forcing*. Mill Hill CA: The Sociology Press.

Glaser, B. G. (2002) 'Constructivist grounded theory?', *Forum Qualitative Sozialforschung/Forum: Qualitative Social Research (2002), Subjectivity and Reflexivity in Qualitative Research I*, vol. 3, no. 3. ART12.

Glaser, B. G. and Strauss, A. (1965) *Awareness of dying*. New York: Aldine Publishing Company.

Glaser, B. G. and Strauss, A. (1967) *The discovery of grounded theory: strategies for qualitative research*. London: Aldine Transactions.

Gobo, G. (2006) 'Sampling, representativeness and generalizability', in C. Seale et al. (eds), *Qualitative Research Practice*. London: SAGE.

Goodall, H. and Campbell, E. (2004) 'A city apart', in L. E. Lassiter et al. (eds), *The other side of Middletown*. Walnut Creek: Alta Mira Press.

Gooding, P. (2011) *Consumer Prices Index and Retail Prices Index: The 2011 Basket of Goods and Services*. Newport: Office of National Statistics.

Gorard, S. (2007) *Quantitative methods in social science*. London: Continuum.

Greenhalgh, T. (2008) 'New methodologies for systematic review', <*www.cochranechildhealth.ualberta.ca/.../Greenhalgh_New%20methodologies%20for%20systematic%20review.pdf,*> accessed February 2010.

Greenhalgh, T., Humphrey, C., Hughes, J., Macfarlane, F., Butler, C. and Pawson, R. (2009) 'How do you modernize a health service? A realist evaluation of whole-scale transformation in London', *Milbank Quarterly*, vol. 87, no. 2, pp. 391–416.

Greenhalgh, T., Russel, J., Ashcroft, R. E. and Parsons, W. (2011) 'Why national health programs need dead philosophers: Wittgensteinian reflections on policymakers' reluctance to learn from history', *Milbank Quarterly*, vol. 98, no. 4, pp. 533–563.

Gubrium, J. F. and Holstein, J. A. (1987) 'The private image: experiential location and method in family studies', *Journal of Marriage and Family*, vol. 49, pp. 773–786.

Gubrium, J. F. and Holstein, J. A. (1997) *The new language of qualitative methods*. Oxford: Oxford University Press.

Guest, G., Bunce, A. and Johnson, L. (2006) 'How many interviews are enough? An experiment with data saturation and variability', *Field Methods*, vol. 18, pp. 59–82.

Guest, G., Bunce, A., Johnson, L., Akumatey, B. and Adeokun, L. (2005) 'Fear, hope and social desirability bias among women at high risk for HIV in West Africa', *Journal of Family Reproductive Health Care*, vol. 31, no. 4, pp. 285–287.

Hammersley, M. (1989) *The dilemma of qualitative method: Herbert Blumer and the Chicago tradition*. London: SAGE.

Hammersley, M. (2011) *Methodology: who needs it?* London: SAGE.

Hammersley, M. and Traianou, A. (2012) *Ethics in qualitative research: controversies and contexts*. London: SAGE.

Harvey, D. (2009) 'Complexity and the case', in D. Byrne and C. Ragin (eds), *The Sage Handbook of Case-Based Methods*. London: SAGE.

Henwood, K. and Pidgeon, N. (2003) 'Grounded theory in psychological research', in P. M. Camic, J. E. Rhodes and L. Yardley (eds), *Qualitative Research in Psychology*. Washington DC: American Psychological Association.

Hume, D. (1949) *A treatise on human nature*. London: J M Dent & Sons.

Igo, S. E. (2007) *The averaged American*. Harvard: Harvard University Press.

Kuzel, A. J. (1999) 'Sampling in qualitative inquiry', in B. F. Crabtree and W. L. Miller (eds), *Doing Qualitative Research*. London: SAGE, pp. 33–46.

Lakatos, I. (1976) *Proofs and refutations: the logic of mathematical discovery*. Cambridge: Cambridge University Press.

Lanchester, J. (2012) 'Why the super-rich love the UK (clue: it's not the weather)', *The Guardian*, 25.02.12, pp. 24–30.

Lassiter, L. E. (2004) 'The story of a collaborative project', in L. E. Lassiter et al. (eds), *The other side of Middletown*. Walnut Creek: Alta Mira Press.

Lassiter, L. E. (2012) 'To fill in the missing piece of the Middletown puzzle: lessons from re-studying Middletown', *The Sociological Review*, vol. 60, no. 3, pp. 421–437.

Letherby, G., Scott, J. and Williams, M. (2013) *Objectivity and subjectivity in social research*. London: SAGE.

Lincoln, Y. S. and Guba, E. G. (1985) *Naturalistic inquiry*. Beverly Hills: SAGE.

Lincoln, Y. S. and Guba, E. G. (2007) 'The only generalization is: there is no generalization', in R. Gomm, M. Hammersley and P. Foster (eds), *Case Study Method*. London: SAGE.

Lindesmith, A. R. (1968) *Addiction and opiates*. Chicago: Aldine Publishing Company.

Lynd, R. S. and Merrell Lynd, H. (1929) *Middletown: a study of modern American culture*. London: Harcourt Brace and Company.

Lynd, R. S. and Merrell Lynd, H. (1937) *Middletown in transition: a study in cultural conflicts*. London: Harcourt Brace Jovanovich Publisher.

MacKenzie, R., Stuart, M., Forde, C., Greenwood, I. and Gardiner, J. (2006) '"All that is solid?" Class, identity and the maintenance of collective orientation amongst redundant steelworkers', *Sociology*, vol. 40, no. 5, pp. 833–852.

March, J. G., Sproull, L. S. and Tamuz, M. (2003) 'Learning from samples of one or fewer', *Quality and Safety in Health Care*, vol. 12, pp. 465–472.

Marsh, C. (1982) *The survey method: the contribution of surveys to sociological explanation*. London: George Allen & Unwin.

Mason, J. (1996) *Qualitative Researching*. London: SAGE.

Mason, J. (2002) *Qualitative Researching*. Second Edition. London: SAGE.

Mason, J. (2007) '"Re-using" qualitative data: on the merits of an investigative epistemology', *Sociological Research Online*, vol. 12, no. 3, p. 3.

Mason, M. (2010) 'Sample size and saturation in PhD studies using qualitative interviews', *Forum Qualitative Sozialforschung/Forum: Qualitative Social Research*, vol. 11, no. 3.

Maxwell, J. A. (2012) *A realist approach to qualitative research*. London: SAGE.

May, T. and Perry, B. (2011) *Social research and reflexivity: content, consequence and context*. London: SAGE.

Melia, K. M. (1996) 'Rediscovering Glaser', *Qualitative Health Research*, vol. 6, no. 3, pp. 368–378.

Merton, R. K. (1968) *Social theory and social structure*. London: Free Press.

Miles, M. B. and Huberman, A. M. (1994) *Qualitative data analysis : an expanded sourcebook*. London: SAGE.

Mill, J. S. (2005) A *system of logic, ratiocinative and inductive*. London: Elibron Classics.

Morse, J. (1995) 'The significance of saturation', *Qualitative Health Research*, vol. 5, no. 2, pp. 147–149.

Morse, J. M. (1991) 'Strategies for sampling', in J. M. Morse (ed.), *Qualitative nursing research: a contemporary dialogue*. London: SAGE.

Morse, J. M. (1994) 'Going in "blind"', *Qualitative Health Research*, vol. 4, no. 1, pp. 3–5.

Morse, J. M. (2007) 'Sampling in grounded theory', in A. Bryant and K. Charmaz (eds), *The SAGE handbook of grounded theory*. London: SAGE.

Moses, Y. T. (2004) 'Forward', in L. E. Lassiter et al. (eds), *The other side of Middletown*. Walnut Creek: Alta Mira Press.

Oliver, C. (2012) 'Critical Realist Grounded Theory: A New Approach for Social Work Research', *British Journal of Social Work*. vol. 42, no. 3, pp. 371–387.

Olsen, W. (2004) 'Methodological triangulation and realist research: an Indian exemplar', in B. Carter and C. New (eds), *Making realism work: realist social theory and empirical research*. London: Routledge.

O'Reilly, M. and Parker, N. (2012) '"Unsatisfactory saturation": a critical exploration of the notion of saturated sample sizes in qualitative research', *Qualitative Research*. Online publication.

Osbourne, T. and Rose, N. (1999) 'Do the social sciences create phenomena? The example of public opinion research', *British Journal of Sociology*, vol. 50, no. 3, pp. 367–396.

Ostrander, S. A. (1993) '"Surely you're not in this just to be helpful" Access, rapport, and interviews in three studies of elites', *Journal of Contemporary Ethnography*, vol. 22, no. 1, pp. 7–27.

Patton, M. Q. (1990) *Qualitative research and evaluation methods. Second Edition.* London: SAGE.

Patton, M. Q. (2002) *Qualitative research and evaluation methods. Third Edition.* London: SAGE.

Pawson, R. (1989) *A measure for measures: a manifesto for empirical sociology.* London: Routledge.

Pawson, R. (2006) *Evidence-based policy: a realist perspective.* London: SAGE.

Pawson, R. (2013) *The science of evaluation: a realist manifesto.* London: SAGE.

Pawson, R. and Tilley, N. (1997) *Realistic Evaluation.* London: SAGE.

Plummer, K. (1983) *Documents of life: an introduction to the problems and literature of a humanistic method.* London: Allen and Unwin.

Ragin, C. (1992a) '"Casing" and the process of social inquiry', in C. Ragin and H. Becker (eds), *What is a case?* Cambridge: Cambridge University Press.

Ragin, C. (1992b) 'Cases of "What is a case?"', in C. Ragin and H. Becker (eds), *What is a case?* Cambridge: Cambridge University Press.

Ragin, C. and Becker, H. S. (1992) *What is a case?* Cambridge: Cambridge University Press.

Rist, R. C. (1981) 'On what we know (or think we do): gatekeeping and the social control of knowledge', in T. S. Popkewitz and B. R. Tabchnick (eds). New York: Praeger.

Rose, G. (1997) 'Situating knowledges: positionality, reflexivities and other tactics', *Progress in Human Geography*, vol. 21, no. 3, pp. 305–320.

Rota, G.-C. (1991) 'The pernicious influence of mathematics upon philosophy', *Synthese*, vol. 88, pp. 165–178.

Rottenberg, D. (1997) *Middletown Jews: the tenuous survival of an American Jewish community.* Bloomington: Indiana University Press.

Savage, M. (2010) *Identities and social change in Britain since 1940: the politics of method.* Oxford: Oxford University Press.

Savage, M., Bagnall, G. and Longhurst, B. (2005) *Globalization and belonging.* London: SAGE.

Sayer, A. (1981) 'Abstraction: a realist interpretation', *Radical Philosophy*, vol. 28, no. 2, pp. 6–15.

Sayer, A. (1992) *Method in social science.* London: Routledge.

Sayer, A. (2000) *Realism and social science.* London: SAGE.

Scambler, G. (2013) 'Resistance in unjust times: Archer, structured agency and the sociology of health inequalities', *Sociology*, vol. 47, no. 1, pp. 142–156.

Seale, C. (1999) *The quality of qualitative research.* London: SAGE.

Smith, D. M. (2005) *On the margins of inclusion: changing labour markets and social exclusion in London.* Bristol: The Policy Press.

Snow, J. (1855) *On the Mode of Communication of Cholera.* UCLA Department of Epidemiology, School of Public Health, <http://www.ph.ucla.edu/epi/snow/snowbook.html>.

Stake, R. (2008) 'Qualitative case studies', in N. K. Denzin and Y. S. Lincoln (eds), *Strategies of qualitative inquiry.* London: SAGE.

Strauss, A. and Corbin, J. (1990) *Basics of qualitative research.* London: SAGE.

Thomson, R. and Holland, J. (2003) 'Hindsight, foresight and insight: the challenges of longitudinal qualitative research', *International Journal of Social Research Methods – Special issue on Longitudinal Qualitative Methods*, vol. 6, no. 3, pp. 233–244.

Uprichard, E. (2013a) 'Describing description (and keeping causality): the case of academic articles on food and eating', *Sociology*, vol. 47, no. 2, pp. 368–382.

Uprichard, E. (2013b) 'Sampling: bridging probability and non-probability designs', *International Journal of Social Research Methodology*, vol. 16, no. 1, pp. 1–11.

Wacquant, L. J. D. (1998) 'Inside the zone: the social art of the hustler in the Black American ghetto', *Theory, Culture and Society*, vol. 15, no. 2, pp. 1–36.

Walton, J. (1992) 'Making a theoretical case', in C. Ragin and H. S. Becker (eds), *What is a case? Exploring the foundations of social inquiry*. Cambridge: Cambridge University Press, pp. 121–138.

Whyte, W. F. (1994) *Street corner society*. Chicago: University of Chicago Press.

Williams, M. (2000) 'Interpretivism and generalisation', *Sociology*, vol. 34, no. 2, pp. 209–224.

Wolfe, A. (1996) *One nation, after all: what middle class Americans really think about god / country / family / racism / welfare / immigration / homosexuality / work / the Left / the Right and each other*. New York: Viking.

Wright Mills, C. (1959) *The sociological imagination*. London: Oxford University Press.

Wuest, J., Merritt-Gray, M., Berman, H. and Ford-Gilobe, M. (2002) 'Illuminating social determinants of women's health using grounded theory', *Health Care for Women International*, vol. 23, pp. 794–808.

Yin, R. K. (2009) *Case study research: design and methods*. London: SAGE.

Znaniecki, F. (1934) *The method of sociology*. New York: Farrar and Reinhart.

Zuckerman, H. (1972) 'Interviewing an ultra-elite', *Public Opinion Quarterly*, vol. 36, no. 2, pp. 159–175.

INDEX

Abbott, A., 90
abduction, 30
abused women, 84–5
academic freedom, 91
access to research subjects, 121–3, 126–7, 131–3
ad hoc sampling, 62
American Anthropological Association, 135
analytic induction, 4, 6, 56–8, 64, 101, 109–10, 127, 139
arbitrary decisions in the course of research, 129
Archer, Margaret, 6, 72–3, 144
Arendt, Hannah, 160
Atkinson, Paul, 151
axial coding, 23–4, 84

Bagnall, Gaynor, 77–8
banking system, 82
Becker, Howard, 110, 144
Benjamin, Walter, 160
Bertaux, Daniel, 45–6, 139
Bertaux-Wiame, Isabelle, 45–6, 139
Bhaskar, Roy, 5, 72–3, 101
bias in sample selection, 124
Blaikie, Norman, 60, 62
Blumer, Herbert, 12, 98–9, 103
Bott, Elizabeth, 96, 124–5
Boudon, Raymond, 87, 144
Bourdieu, Pierre, 77, 124, 143–4
Bourgois, Phillipe, 141–2
Bowley, Sir Arthur Lyon, 1
bread-making, 45–6
Brody, Howard, 71
Browne, Angela, 37–9
Browne, Kath, 131–3
Bryant, Antony, 30
Bunce, Arwan, 147–52
Burawoy, Michael, 95
Byrne, David, 97

call centres, 101
Campbell, Donald T., 139
Campbell, Elizabeth, 93

Carter, Bob, 81
case selection, 69, 83–5, 100, 121, 124, 134, 141, 155, 157–60; purposeful approach to, 107–20
case studies, 107–10
'casing' methodology, 7, 73, 107–12, 117–20, 135, 154, 159–60
caste system, 77
causality, process approach to, 99
chain sampling, 40, 131, 134; *see also* snowball sampling
Charmaz, Kathy, 2, 4, 25–6, 29–30, 83–4, 152
cholera, 69–71
Chorlton, 102
Clark, Andrew, 125
Clark, Tom, 122
Clarke, Adele, 29
class divisions, 125, 137–8
co-construction of theory, 31, 132–3, 152
coding of data, 13, 15; *see also* axial coding; open coding
Coffey, Amanda, 151
confirming and *disconfirming* cases, 41–2
constant comparison, 14–18, 21, 25
constructivism, 3–4, 28–31, 64, 83–4, 96, 152
convenience sampling, 1, 3, 27, 35, 42, 80
Cooper, Edmund, 70–1
Corbin, Juliet, 2–3, 18–25, 28, 33, 100, 147
credibility of research, 41–2
Creswell, J., 146
criterion sampling, 40
critical-case sampling, 39–40, 64

Danermark, Berth, 81–2
Daston, Lorraine, 63
data mining, 140
Davies, Katherine, 129–30
demographic characteristics used in sample selection, 26–7
deviant-case sampling, 37–8
Dey, I., 151
dialogue between researcher and research subject, 30